RICHARD III

William Shakespeare

EDITORIAL DIRECTOR Justin Kestler
EXECUTIVE EDITOR Ben Florman
DIRECTOR OF TECHNOLOGY Tammy Hepps

SERIES EDITORS Boomie Aglietti, John Crowther, Justin Kestler
MANAGING EDITOR Vince Janoski

WRITERS Susannah Mandel, Brian Phillips
EDITORS John Crowther, Benjamin Morgan

This edition published by Spark Publishing

Spark Publishing
A Division of SparkNotes LLC
120 Fifth Avenue, 8th Floor
New York, NY 10011

Any book purchased without a cover is stolen property, reported as "unsold and destroyed" to the Publisher, who receives no payment for such "stripped books."

Please submit all comments and questions or report errors to www.sparknotes.com/errors

Library of Congress Catalog-in-Publication Data available upon request

Printed and bound in the United States

ISBN 1-58663-486-0

A Prologue from the Bard

Brave scholars, blessed with time and energy,
    At school, fair Harvard, set about to glean,
From dusty tomes and modern poetry,
    All truths and knowledge formerly unseen.
From forth the hungry minds of these good folk
    Study guides, star-floss'd, soon came to life;
Whose deep and deft analysis awoke
    The latent "A"s of those in lit'rary strife.
Aim far past passing—insight from our trove
    Will free your comprehension from its cage.
Our SparkNotes' worth, online we also prove;
    Behold this book! Same brains, but paper page.
If patient or "whatever," please attend,
    What you have missed, our toil shall strive to mend.

CONTENTS

CONTEXT

THE MOST INFLUENTIAL WRITER in all of English literature, William Shakespeare was born in 1564 to a successful middle-class glove-maker in Stratford-upon-Avon, England. Shakespeare attended grammar school, but his formal education proceeded no further. In 1582 he married an older woman, Anne Hathaway, and had three children with her. Around 1590 he left his family behind and traveled to London to work as an actor and playwright. Public and critical acclaim quickly followed, and Shakespeare eventually became the most popular playwright in England and part-owner of the Globe Theater. His career bridged the reigns of Elizabeth I (ruled 1558–1603) and James I (ruled 1603–1625), and he was a favorite of both monarchs. Indeed, James granted Shakespeare's company the greatest possible compliment by bestowing upon its members the title of King's Men. Wealthy and renowned, Shakespeare retired to Stratford and died in 1616 at the age of fifty-two. At the time of Shakespeare's death, literary luminaries such as Ben Jonson hailed his works as timeless.

Shakespeare's works were collected and printed in various editions in the century following his death, and by the early eighteenth century his reputation as the greatest poet ever to write in English was well established. The unprecedented admiration garnered by his works led to a fierce curiosity about Shakespeare's life, but the dearth of biographical information has left many details of Shakespeare's personal history shrouded in mystery. Some people have concluded from this fact and from Shakespeare's modest education that Shakespeare's plays were actually written by someone else—Francis Bacon and the earl of Oxford are the two most popular candidates—but the support for this claim is overwhelmingly circumstantial, and the theory is not taken seriously by many scholars.

In the absence of credible evidence to the contrary, Shakespeare must be viewed as the author of the thirty-seven plays and 154 sonnets that bear his name. The legacy of this body of work is immense. A number of Shakespeare's plays seem to have transcended even the category of brilliance, becoming so influential as to affect profoundly the course of Western literature and culture ever after.

Richard III belongs to the genre of Shakespeare's plays known as the histories, which deal with events in England's historical past after the Norman Conquest, in 1066. Although it is often viewed as a sequel to three of Shakespeare's earlier history plays—1 Henry VI, 2 Henry VI, and 3 *Henry VI*—*Richard III* is usually read and performed on its own. The play chronicles the bloody deeds and atrocities perpetrated by its central figure—the murderous and tyrannical King Richard III. Richard invites an eerie fascination, and generations of readers have found themselves seduced by his brilliance with words and his persuasive emotional manipulations even as they are repelled by his evil.

But Richard is difficult to understand psychologically because, while he is clearly power-hungry and sadistic, the deep-rooted motivations for his malevolent hatred are hard to pinpoint. Some critics feel that Richard is not really a fully developed character in the way that Shakespeare's later characters, such as Macbeth or Hamlet, are. Such critics argue that Richard does not possess a complex human psychology but instead recalls a stock character from early medieval drama. Like the "Vice" character of medieval morality pageants, who simply represented the evil in man, Richard does not justify his villainy—he is simply bad. Indeed, Richard, with self-conscious theatricality, compares himself to this standard character when he says, "Thus like the formal Vice, Iniquity, / I moralize two meanings in one word" (III.i.82–83). We should note that the mere fact that he reflects upon his similarity to the Vice figure suggests that there is more to him than this mere resemblance. Watching Richard's character, Shakespeare's audiences also would have thought of the "Machiavel," the archetype of the scandalously amoral, power-hungry ruler that had been made famous by the Renaissance Italian writer Niccolò Machiavelli in *The Prince* (first published in 1532).

Bloody though he was, nevertheless, the historical King Richard III was not necessarily more murderous than the kings who preceded or succeeded him. Nor is it likely that he was deformed, as Shakespeare portrays him. Winners, not losers, write history. When Shakespeare wrote this play, Queen Elizabeth I ruled England; Elizabeth was a descendant of King Henry VII, the ruler who overthrew Richard. Thus, the official party line of the Elizabethan era was that Richard was a monster who was not a legitimate ruler of England. It would have been thoroughly dangerous for Shakespeare to suggest otherwise.

HISTORY, BACKGROUND, AND FAMILY LINES

For a number of decades in the late fifteenth century, England's royal family was locked in a power struggle that periodically erupted into violence. Historians have labeled this battle the Wars of the Roses, after the family symbols of the two contending groups: the Lancaster family, symbolized by a red rose, and the York family, symbolized by a white one.

The problems began in the late fourteenth century, with the death of the long-lived King Edward III, of the house of Plantagenet. Edward III had seven sons, of whom the fourth and fifth became the fathers of dynasties. The elder was called John of Gaunt, the duke of Lancaster, and his younger brother was called Edmund of Langley, duke of York. Their descendants formed two important clans—the Lancasters and the Yorks. Both clans derived from royal blood, and both produced ambitious men who were willing to fight for the throne. The Lancasters and their allies are sometimes called the Lancastrians; the Yorks and their allies are called the Yorkists.

After the death of Edward III, King Richard II—who was descended from Edward's eldest son, and was thus neither a York nor a Lancaster—ruled for twenty-two years. However, he was soon overthrown by his cousin (the son of John of Gaunt), a Lancaster named Henry Bolingbroke who became Henry IV. Henry IV was in turn succeeded by his son, Henry V, who was succeeded by his son, Henry VI.

But in the late fifteenth century, fighting broke out again, this time between Lancasters and Yorks. After a bloody struggle, the Lancastrian Henry VI was deposed in 1461, and the head of the house of York took the throne as King Edward IV. Henry VI briefly resumed the kingship in 1470, but again he was deposed, and, this time, he was killed, along with his son and destined heir, who was known as Edward, prince of Wales (a title always given to the current heir to the throne). They were murdered by the sons of the York family: King Edward IV, Clarence, and their younger brother Richard. After the executions, Edward took the throne once again. The action of *Richard III* begins shortly after this event, but in reality the hostility between the two families was much older. The Lancastrians had killed a second York son—Edmund, earl of Rutland—when he was still quite young. (Shakespeare's other history plays—*Richard II, Henry IV Parts One & Two, Henry V,* and *Henry VI*

Parts One, Two, & Three—cover all of these events.) Shakespeare often plays fast and loose with the facts, stretching and altering the timeline to suit his dramatic purposes, but the plays generally are based upon historical records.

The events of this civil war—including the murders of King Henry and Prince Edward by the York brothers, and the earlier killing of the Earl of Rutland by Henry's family—are important background to *Richard III*. In Shakespeare's version, for one thing, both Henry and Edward leave widows: Henry's is the former Queen Margaret, who bitterly curses the Yorks in Act I, scene iii; Edward's is Lady Anne, who mourns his death and that of Henry in Act I, scene ii, and who later becomes Richard's wife.

When the action of *Richard III* begins, Edward IV and his brothers have overthrown the Lancastrians, but Edward is growing older and is often sick. His malicious and slightly deformed younger brother, Richard, is power-hungry and is plotting to get his hands on the throne. However, a great many people stand between him and the kingship. For example, even when King Edward himself dies, he will leave behind two sons who are in line for the throne: the young Prince Edward, the crown prince, and his brother, the young duke of York. Fortunately for Richard's purposes, they are still children, and they meet their final fate as the unfortunate "princes in the Tower." The mother of the princes is Queen Elizabeth, of the Woodeville family, and she has powerful and intelligent kinsmen who will try to protect her and her children, thus making the queen's kin yet another threat to Richard. The royal couple also has a daughter, young Elizabeth, who will later become an important pawn in royal marriage negotiations.

In addition to all of these obstacles to the throne, Richard's trusting elder brother, the duke of Clarence, also blocks Richard's road to power. Richard must dispose of Clarence in order to clear the line of descent and seize the throne. Finally, Richard finds himself under threat from an unexpected source: Henry Tudor, the earl of Richmond, a descendant of a secondary branch of the Lancasters (from John of Gaunt's third wife), has been gathering power overseas. Richmond feels that he has a claim to the throne for which he is willing to challenge Richard—setting us up for the final showdown between the Houses of York and Lancaster at the Battle of Bosworth Field.

PLOT OVERVIEW

AFTER A LONG CIVIL WAR between the royal family of York and the royal family of Lancaster, England enjoys a period of peace under King Edward IV and the victorious Yorks. But Edward's younger brother, Richard, resents Edward's power and the happiness of those around him. Malicious, power-hungry, and bitter about his physical deformity, Richard begins to aspire secretly to the throne—and decides to kill anyone he has to in order to become king.

Using his intelligence and his skills of deception and political manipulation, Richard begins his campaign for the throne. He manipulates a noblewoman, Lady Anne, into marrying him—even though she knows that he murdered her first husband. He has his own older brother, Clarence, executed, and shifts the burden of guilt onto his sick older brother King Edward in order to accelerate Edward's illness and death. After King Edward dies, Richard becomes lord protector of England—the figure in charge until the elder of Edward's two sons grows up.

Next Richard kills the court noblemen who are loyal to the princes, most notably Lord Hastings, the lord chamberlain of England. He then has the boys' relatives on their mother's side—the powerful kinsmen of Edward's wife, Queen Elizabeth—arrested and executed. With Elizabeth and the princes now unprotected, Richard has his political allies, particularly his right-hand man, Lord Buckingham, campaign to have Richard crowned king. Richard then imprisons the young princes in the Tower and, in his bloodiest move yet, sends hired murderers to kill both children.

By this time, Richard's reign of terror has caused the common people of England to fear and loathe him, and he has alienated nearly all the noblemen of the court—even the power-hungry Buckingham. When rumors begin to circulate about a challenger to the throne who is gathering forces in France, noblemen defect in droves to join his forces. The challenger is the earl of Richmond, a descendant of a secondary arm of the Lancaster family, and England is ready to welcome him.

Richard, in the meantime, tries to consolidate his power. He has his wife, Queen Anne, murdered, so that he can marry young Elizabeth, the daughter of the former Queen Elizabeth and the dead King Edward. Though young Elizabeth is his niece, the alliance would secure his claim to the throne. Nevertheless, Richard has begun to lose control of events, and Queen Elizabeth manages to forestall him. Meanwhile, she secretly promises to marry young Elizabeth to Richmond.

Richmond finally invades England. The night before the battle that will decide everything, Richard has a terrible dream in which the ghosts of all the people he has murdered appear and curse him, telling him that he will die the next day. In the battle on the following morning, Richard is killed, and Richmond is crowned King Henry VII. Promising a new era of peace for England, the new king is betrothed to young Elizabeth in order to unite the warring houses of Lancaster and York.

CHARACTER LIST

Richard   Also called the duke of Gloucester, and eventually crowned King Richard III. Deformed in body and twisted in mind, Richard is both the central character and the villain of the play. He is evil, corrupt, sadistic, and manipulative, and he will stop at nothing to become king. His intelligence, political brilliance, and dazzling use of language keep the audience fascinated—and his subjects and rivals under his thumb.

Buckingham   Richard's right-hand man in his schemes to gain power. The duke of Buckingham is almost as amoral and ambitious as Richard himself.

King Edward IV   The older brother of Richard and Clarence, and the king of England at the start of the play. Edward was deeply involved in the Yorkists' brutal overthrow of the Lancaster regime, but as king he is devoted to achieving a reconciliation among the various political factions of his reign. He is unaware that Richard attempts to thwart him at every turn.

Clarence   The gentle, trusting brother born between Edward and Richard in the York family. Richard has Clarence murdered in order to get him out of the way. Clarence leaves two children, a son and a daughter.

Queen Elizabeth   The wife of King Edward IV and the mother of the two young princes (the heirs to the throne) and their older sister, young Elizabeth. After Edward's death, Queen Elizabeth (also called Lady Gray) is at Richard's mercy. Richard rightly views her as an enemy because she opposes his rise to power, and because she is intelligent and fairly strong-willed. Elizabeth is part of the Woodeville family; her kinsmen—Dorset, Rivers, and Gray—are her allies in the court.

Dorset, Rivers, and Gray The kinsmen and allies of Elizabeth, and members of the Woodeville and Gray families. Rivers is Elizabeth's brother, while Gray and Dorset are her sons from her first marriage. Richard eventually executes Rivers and Gray, but Dorset flees and survives.

Anne The young widow of Prince Edward, who was the son of the former king, Henry VI. Lady Anne hates Richard for the death of her husband, but for reasons of politics—and for sadistic pleasure—Richard persuades Anne to marry him.

Duchess of York Widowed mother of Richard, Clarence, and King Edward IV. The duchess of York is Elizabeth's mother-in-law, and she is very protective of Elizabeth and her children, who are the duchess's grandchildren. She is angry with, and eventually curses, Richard for his heinous actions.

Margaret Widow of the dead King Henry VI, and mother of the slain Prince Edward. In medieval times, when kings were deposed, their children were often killed to remove any threat from the royal line of descent—but their wives were left alive because they were considered harmless. Margaret was the wife of the king before Edward, the Lancastrian Henry VI, who was subsequently deposed and murdered (along with their children) by the family of King Edward IV and Richard. She is embittered and hates both Richard and the people he is trying to get rid of, all of whom were complicit in the destruction of the Lancasters.

The princes The two young sons of King Edward IV and his wife, Elizabeth, their names are actually Prince Edward and the young duke of York, but they are often referred to collectively. Agents of Richard murder these boys— Richard's nephews—in the Tower of London. Young Prince Edward, the rightful heir to the throne, should not be confused with the elder Edward, prince of Wales (the first husband of Lady Anne, and the son of the former king, Henry VI.), who was killed before the play begins.

Young Elizabeth The former Queen Elizabeth's daughter. Young Elizabeth enjoys the fate of many Renaissance noblewomen. She becomes a pawn in political power-brokering, and is promised in marriage at the end of the play to Richmond, the Lancastrian rebel leader, in order to unite the warring houses of York and Lancaster.

Ratcliffe, Catesby Two of Richard's flunkies among the nobility.

Tyrrell A murderer whom Richard hires to kill his young cousins, the princes in the Tower of London.

Richmond A member of a branch of the Lancaster royal family. Richmond gathers a force of rebels to challenge Richard for the throne. He is meant to represent goodness, justice, and fairness—all the things Richard does not. Richmond is portrayed in such a glowing light in part because he founded the Tudor dynasty, which still ruled England in Shakespeare's day.

Hastings A lord who maintains his integrity, remaining loyal to the family of King Edward IV. Hastings winds up dead for making the mistake of trusting Richard.

Stanley The stepfather of Richmond. Lord Stanley, earl of Derby, secretly helps Richmond, although he cannot escape Richard's watchful gaze.

Lord Mayor of London A gullible and suggestible fellow whom Richard and Buckingham use as a pawn in their ploy to make Richard king.

Vaughan A friend of Elizabeth, Dorset, Rivers, and Gray who is executed by Richard along with Rivers and Grey.

ANALYSIS OF MAJOR CHARACTERS

RICHARD III

Richard is in every way the dominant character of the play that bears his name, to the extent that he is both the protagonist of the story and its major villain. *Richard III* is an intense exploration of the psychology of evil, and that exploration is centered on Richard's mind. Critics sometimes compare Richard to the medieval character, Vice, who was a flat and one-sided embodiment of evil. However, especially in the later scenes of the play, Richard proves to be highly self-reflective and complicated—making his heinous acts all the more chilling.

Perhaps more than in any other play by Shakespeare, the audience of *Richard III* experiences a complex, ambiguous, and highly changeable relationship with the main character. Richard is clearly a villain—he declares outright in his very first speech that he intends to stop at nothing to achieve his nefarious designs. But despite his open allegiance to evil, he is such a charismatic and fascinating figure that, for much of the play, we are likely to sympathize with him, or at least to be impressed with him. In this way, our relationship with Richard mimics the other characters' relationships with him, conveying a powerful sense of the force of his personality. Even characters such as Lady Anne, who have an explicit knowledge of his wickedness, allow themselves to be seduced by his brilliant wordplay, his skillful argumentation, and his relentless pursuit of his selfish desires.

Richard's long, fascinating monologues, in which he outlines his plans and gleefully confesses all his evil thoughts, are central to the audience's experience of Richard. Shakespeare uses these monologues brilliantly to control the audience's impression of Richard, enabling this manipulative protagonist to work his charms on the audience. In Act I, scene i, for example, Richard dolefully claims that his malice toward others stems from the fact that he is unloved, and that he is unloved because of his physical deformity. This claim, which casts the other characters of the play as villains for punishing

Richard for his appearance, makes it easy to sympathize with Richard during the first scenes of the play.

It quickly becomes apparent, however, that Richard simply uses his deformity as a tool to gain the sympathy of others—including us. Richard's evil is a much more innate part of his character than simple bitterness about his ugly body. But he uses this speech to win our trust, and he repeats this ploy throughout his struggle to be crowned king. After he is crowned king and Richmond begins his uprising, Richard's monologues end. Once Richard stops exerting his charisma on the audience, his real nature becomes much more apparent, and by the end of the play he can be seen for the monster that he is.

THE PRINCES

The most famous crime of the historical Richard III, and the deed for which he was most demonized in the century following his death, is his murder of the two young princes in the Tower of London. For centuries after the death of Edward IV, the fate of the princes was a mystery—all that was known was that they had disappeared. It was speculated that Richard had them killed, it was speculated that they had spent their entire lives as prisoners in the tower, and it was speculated that they had escaped and lived abroad. The English author Sir Thomas More wrote that they were killed and buried at the foot of a staircase in the White Tower. Many years later, in 1674, workers in the Tower of London discovered two tiny skeletons hidden in a chest buried beneath a staircase of the tower. The skeletons date from approximately the late fifteenth century, and serve as the best evidence that the young sons of Edward IV were in fact murdered in the tower. There is still no conclusive proof that it was Richard who had them murdered—some scholars even think it could have been Richmond. Still, thanks to popular legend, Shakespeare's play, and the biography of Richard that More wrote a few years before the play, Richard has gone down in history as the most likely culprit.

Because the story of the princes in the tower was so well known, it was crucial to *Richard III* that Shakespeare make the princes memorable and engaging figures despite their youth and their relatively small roles in the story. As a result, Shakespeare creates princes who are highly intelligent—they are among the only characters in the play to see through Richard's scheme entirely. They are courageous, standing up fearlessly to the powerful Richard. They are charismatic, outdoing Richard in games of wordplay. However, they are utterly, pitifully helpless because they are so young. Though Elizabeth remarks that her younger son is a "parlous boy," meaning sharp or mischievous, the princes are never a threat to Richard, and they are unable to defend themselves against him (II.iv.35). Yet Shakespeare creates the sense that, had the princes lived, they would have grown up to become more than a match for their wicked uncle.

MARGARET

Though she plays a very minor role in the play's plot, mostly prowling around the castle cursing to herself, Margaret is nevertheless one of the most important and memorable characters in *Richard III*. The impotent, overpowering rage that she directs at Richard and his family stands for the helpless, righteous anger of all Richard's victims. The curses she levels at the royals in Act I, which are among the most startling and memorable in all of Shakespeare, foreshadow and essentially determine future events of the play. Her lesson to Elizabeth and the duchess about how to curse paints a striking picture of the psychology of victimization and the use of language as a means of alleviating anguish.

As the wife of the dead and vanquished King Henry VI, Margaret also represents the plight of women under the patriarchal power structure of Renaissance England. Without a husband to grant her status and security, she is reduced to depending on the charity of her family's murderers to survive—a dire situation that she later wishes on Elizabeth. Margaret is a one-dimensional character, representing rage and pain, but she is vital to the play for the sheer focus of torment she brings to the world surrounding Richard's irresistible evil.

THEMES, MOTIFS & SYMBOLS

THEMES

Themes are the fundamental and often universal ideas explored in a literary work.

THE ALLURE OF EVIL

When Richard claims that his deformity is the cause of his wicked ways, he seems to be manipulating us for sympathy, just as he manipulates the other characters throughout the play. As a result, *Richard III* does not explore the cause of evil in the human mind so much as it explores its operation, depicting the workings of Richard's mind and the methods he uses to manipulate, control, and injure others for his own gain. Central to this aspect of the play is the idea that Richard's victims are complicit in their own destruction. Just as Lady Anne allows herself to be seduced by Richard, even knowing that he will kill her, other characters allow themselves to be taken in by his charisma and overlook his dishonesty and violent behavior. This tendency is echoed in Richard's relationship with the audience for much of the play. Even though the audience is likely to be repulsed by Richard's actions, his gleeful, brilliant, revealing monologues cause most viewers to like him and even hope that he will succeed despite his obvious malice.

THE CONNECTION BETWEEN RULER AND STATE

The so-called window scenes in *Richard III*—the conversation of the common people in Act II, scene iii; Buckingham's speech to the masses and Richard's acceptance of the crown in Act III; and the scene of the Scrivener in Act III, scene iv—provide a glimpse of how the drama in the royal palace affects the lives of the common people outside its walls. As a history play, *Richard III* is at least somewhat concerned with the consequences of the behavior of those in power, and with ideas of good rulership and governance. It is significant that the common people come to fear and distrust Richard long before most of the nobles in the palace, and that the opposition of the common people to Richard is one of the main forces that enables

Richmond to overthrow him. In these ways, *Richard III* explores a theme Shakespeare later revisited in *Hamlet* and *Macbeth*—the idea that the moral righteousness of a political ruler has a direct bearing on the health of the state. A state with a good ruler will tend to flourish (as Denmark does under King Hamlet), while a state with a bad ruler will tend to suffer (as Scotland does under Macbeth).

THE POWER OF LANGUAGE

An interesting secondary theme of *Richard III* is the power of language, or the importance of language in achieving political power. Language may not always be a necessary instrument of power, but for Richard, it is a crucial weapon. His extraordinary skill with words enables him to manipulate, confuse, and control those around him. Richard's skill with language and argument is what enables him to woo Lady Anne, have Clarence thrown in prison, keep the Woodvilles off his track, blame the king for Clarence's death, and achieve Hastings's execution, all at very little risk to himself. Interestingly, language also seems to be the only defense against Richard, as is shown when the princes match his skill at wordplay and thus indicate their ability to see through his schemes. In such cases, Richard simply uses violence as an expedient and has his enemies, including the princes, put to death.

THE BIRTH OF THE TUDOR DYNASTY

Richard III dramatizes a key turning point in English history: the end of the Wars of the Roses and the rise to power of the Tudor dynasty in the figure of Henry VII. The Tudors continued to rule England in Shakespeare's day—Queen Elizabeth I, who sat on the throne when *Richard III* was written, was a Tudor. As a playwright in sixteenth-century England, Shakespeare had to court the favor of those in power, who literally could make or break his career. As a result, Shakespeare's portrayal of Richard III as a vile, hateful villain is in part designed to set up a glorious ascension for Henry VII at the end of the play. Henry overthrew Richard, after all, and the worse Richard seems, the better Henry will seem for defeating him; moreover, the better Henry seems, the more likely the Tudors are to approve of Shakespeare's play. Had Shakespeare portrayed Richard as a hero, then Henry might have seemed villainous for usurping his throne, and Shakespeare might have fallen from favor with Queen Elizabeth. Of course, these political considerations are by no means the main focus of the play—Shakespeare's exploration of the psychology of evil stands on its own and transcends mere propaganda.

THEMES

Still, it is important to realize that the history Shakespeare recounts in his story was still very much alive when he wrote it, and that the considerations of his own time strongly affected his portrayal of the past.

MOTIFS

Motifs are recurring structures, contrasts, or literary devices that can help to develop and inform the text's major themes.

THE SUPERNATURAL

For a play supposedly based on actual history, *Richard III* involves an extraordinary number of supernatural elements. Some of these elements are Margaret's prophetic curses, Clarence and Stanley's prophetic dreams, the allegations of witchcraft Richard levels at Elizabeth and mistress Shore, the continual association of Richard with devils and demons (for example, he is often called a hell-hound), Richard's comparison of himself to the shape-shifting Proteus, the Princes' discussion of the ghosts of their dead uncles, and—most significant—the parade of eleven ghosts that visits Richard and Richmond the night before the battle. These supernatural elements serve to create an atmosphere of intense dread and gloom that matches the malice and evil of Richard's inner self, and also serve to heighten the sense that Richard's reign is innately evil, transforming England into a kind of Gothic netherworld.

DREAMS

The motif of prophetic dreams is part of the play's larger preoccupation with the supernatural, but the idea of dreams emerges as its own separate motif after Stanley's dream about Hastings's death. Clarence and Stanley both have dreams that not only predict the future, but that are also heavy with important symbolism. For example, Clarence's dream involves Richard causing his drowning at sea. Immediately after it, he is drowned in a cask of wine by murderers hired by Richard. In addition, Stanley's dream involves Hastings being gored by a boar—Richard's heraldic symbol. Immediately after it, Richard orders Hastings's execution.

SYMBOLS

Symbols are objects, characters, figures, or colors used to represent abstract ideas or concepts.

THE BOAR

The boar is Richard's heraldic symbol, and is used several times throughout the play to represent him, most notably in Stanley's dream about Hastings's death. The idea of the boar is also played on in describing Richard's deformity, and Richard is cursed by the duchess as an "abortive, rooting hog" (I.iii.225). The boar was one of the most dangerous animals that people hunted in the Middle Ages and Renaissance, and Shakespeare's audience would have associated it with untamed aggression and uncontrollable violence.

SUMMARY & ANALYSIS

ACT I, SCENE I

...since I cannot prove a lover
To entertain these fair well-spoken days,
I am determined to prove a villain
And hate the idle pleasures of these days.

(See QUOTATIONS, *p. 57)*

SUMMARY

Richard, the duke of Gloucester, speaks in a monologue addressed to himself and to the audience. After a lengthy civil war, he says, peace at last has returned to the royal house of England. Richard says that his older brother, King Edward IV, now sits on the throne, and everyone around Richard is involved in a great celebration. But Richard himself will not join in the festivities. He complains that he was born deformed and ugly, and bitterly laments his bad luck. He vows to make everybody around him miserable as well. Moreover, Richard says, he is power-hungry, and seeks to gain control over the entire court. He implies that his ultimate goal is to make himself king.

Working toward this goal, Richard has set in motion various schemes against the other noblemen of the court. The first victim is Richard's own brother, Clarence. Richard and Clarence are the two younger brothers of the current king, Edward IV, who is very ill and highly suggestible at the moment. Richard says that he has planted rumors to make Edward suspicious of Clarence.

Clarence himself now enters, under armed guard. Richard's rumor-planting has worked, and Clarence is being led to the Tower of London, where English political prisoners were traditionally imprisoned and often executed. Richard, pretending to be very sad to see Clarence made a prisoner, suggests to Clarence that King Edward must have been influenced by his wife, Queen Elizabeth, or by his mistress, Lady Shore, to become suspicious of Clarence. Richard promises that he will try to have Clarence set free. But after Clarence is led offstage toward the Tower, Richard gleefully says to himself that he will make sure Clarence never returns.

Lord Hastings, the lord Chamberlain of the court, now enters. He was earlier imprisoned in the Tower by the suspicious King Edward, but has now been freed. Richard, pretending ignorance, asks Hastings for the latest news, and Hastings tells him that Edward is very sick. After Hastings leaves, Richard gloats over Edward's illness. Edward's death would bring Richard one step closer to the throne. Richard wants Clarence to die first, however, so that Richard will be the legal heir to power. Richard's planned next step is to try to marry a noblewoman named Lady Anne Neville. An alliance with her would help Richard on his way to the throne. Lady Anne recently has been widowed—she was married to the son of the previous king, Henry VI, who recently was deposed and murdered, along with his son, by Richard's family. Anne is thus in deep mourning. But the sadistic and amoral Richard is amused by the idea of persuading her to marry him under these circumstances.

ANALYSIS

In the play's well-known opening lines, Richard refers to events that Shakespeare chronicles in his earlier plays *Henry VI, Parts One, Two, and Three,* and with which he would have expected his viewers to be familiar. The *Henry VI* plays detail an exhausting civil war for the throne of England, which boiled down to a contest between two families: the House of York and the House of Lancaster. This civil war is known as the Wars of the Roses, because of the white and red roses that symbolized the houses of York and of Lancaster, respectively. Richard's side, the House of York, eventually wins, and Richard's oldest brother, Edward, is now King Edward IV.

This knowledge of the recent civil war helps us make sense of the opening lines, spoken by Richard: "Now is the winter of our discontent / Made glorious summer by this son of York; / And all the clouds that loured upon our homes / In the deep bosom of the ocean buried" (I.i.1–4). Richard's brother Edward is the "son of York" who has brought "glorious summer" to the kingdom, and Richard's "winter of our discontent" is the recently ended civil war. The "house" is the House of York, to which Richard and his brothers Edward and Clarence belong, and which now rules the kingdom.

Richard's opening speech explains important elements of his character. He says that because he cannot be happy—in part because he feels that he cannot be sexually successful with women— he has decided to ruin these prosperous times and make everybody else miserable: "[T]herefore since I cannot prove a lover / To entertain these fair well-spoken days, / I am determined to prove a villain / And hate the idle pleasures of these days" (I.i.28–31). He goes on to tell us how he has begun to spread rumors that should cause King Edward to suspect Clarence (Richard, and Edward's brother), and to punish and imprison him—plans whose results become visible when Clarence walks onstage under guard.

But Richard is not really as simple and straightforward as his description of himself implies, however. The true motivations for his evil manipulations remain mysterious. In his speech, he speaks of his bitterness at his deformity; Richard is a hunchback, and has something wrong with one of his arms. But the play's later action shows that Richard is physically very active, and that he is in fact quite confident in his ability to seduce women. Bitterness at his deformity also fails to explain his overpowering desire to be king or his lust for power. For these reasons, Richard may not seem like an entirely realistic and consistent personality to us. Moreover, for Shakespeare's audience, Richard would have been strongly reminiscent of the two-dimensional "Vice" character of medieval morality plays, a character who was meant to illustrate man's evil side rather than to present a psychologically realistic portrait. In fact, Richard explicitly compares himself to Vice (III.i.82). But Richard is much more than this stock figure—Shakespeare consistently creates the impression that there is more to Richard than we can begin to grasp.

Richard's opening monologue also shows us what a masterful speaker he is. His speech is full of striking metaphors and images, such as his pun on "son" when he describes how King Edward has turned winter to summer (I.i.2). Most important, however, this scene shows us the deceptive way in which Richard interacts with the world. Richard has one persona when he speaks alone, but as soon as somebody else comes on stage, his attitude changes. In fact, he lies and manipulates so convincingly that we certainly would believe the sympathy and love he expresses toward his unhappy brother Clarence if we did not hear his earlier vow to destroy Clarence—a vow which he repeats as soon as Clarence leaves the stage. Richard's remarkable skill at self-presentation has intrigued generations of actors and audiences alike. The character Richard is himself an actor, playing a role to the other characters on stage.

Finally, this scene hints at the complicated web of schemes and alliances that grows even more complex during the course of the play. In Richard's scheme against Clarence, we see the first concrete result of his subtle and hypocritical designs. Additionally, in the symmetrical exchange of noblemen going in and out of the Tower of London we see how fleeting favor must have been in the royal court: Clarence falls from royal favor and is locked up, while Hastings regains it and is freed. This unpredictability of fortune and favor was a popular literary theme in Shakespeare's day.

ACT I, SCENE II

SUMMARY

Lady Anne, the widow of King Henry VI's son, Edward, enters the royal castle with a group of men bearing the coffin of Henry VI. She curses Richard for having killed Henry. Both Henry VI and Edward, who were of the House of Lancaster, have recently been killed by members of the House of York, the family of the current king, Edward IV, and Richard. Anne says that Richard is to blame for both deaths. She refers spitefully to her husband's killer as she mourns for the dead king and prince, praying that any child Richard might have be deformed and sick, and that he make any woman he might marry be as miserable as Anne herself is.

Suddenly, Richard himself enters the room. Anne reacts with horror and spite, but Richard orders the attendants to stop the procession so that he can speak with her. He addresses Anne gently, but she curses him as the murderer of her husband and father-in-law. Anne points to the bloody wounds on the corpse of the dead Henry VI, saying that they have started to bleed. (According to Renaissance tradition, the wounds of a murdered person begin to bleed again if the killer comes close to the corpse.)

Praising Anne's gentleness and beauty, Richard begins to court her romantically. Anne naturally reacts with anger and horror and reminds Richard repeatedly that she knows he killed her husband and King Henry. He tells Anne that she ought to forgive him his crime out of Christian charity, then denies that he killed her husband at all. Anne remains angry, but her fierceness seems to dwindle gradually in the face of Richard's eloquence and apparent sincerity. Finally, in a highly theatrical gesture, Richard kneels before her and hands her his sword, telling her to kill him if she will not forgive him, indicating that he doesn't want to live if she hates him. Anne begins to stab toward his chest, but Richard keeps speaking, saying that he killed Henry IV and Edward out of passion for Anne herself— Anne's beauty drove him to it. Anne lowers the sword.

Richard slips his ring onto her finger, telling her that she can make him happy only by forgiving him and becoming his wife. Anne says that she may take the ring but that she will not give him her hand. Richard persists, and Anne agrees to meet him later at a place he names.

As soon as Richard is alone, he gleefully begins to celebrate his conquest of Anne. He asks scornfully whether she has already forgotten her husband, murdered by his (Richard's) hand. He gloats over having won her even while her eyes were still filled with the tears of mourning, and over having manipulated her affections even though she hates him.

ANALYSIS

Act I, scene ii is psychologically complicated, and is without doubt one of the most difficult scenes in the entire play. It is hard for many readers to accept that Anne, who mourns the dead Henry and curses Richard at the beginning of the scene, could possibly wear his ring and let him court her by the scene's end. This scene demonstrates Richard's brilliance as a manipulator of people. We receive a taste of this brilliance in Act I, scene i, but the wooing of Anne shows Richard's persuasive abilities at a whole new level. Richard's ability to persuade the grieving, bitter Anne to accept him as a suitor is surely proof of his ominous skill in playing upon people's emotions and in convincing them that he is sincere when in fact he is lying through his teeth.

Richard manipulates Anne by feigning gentleness and persistently praising her beauty, a technique that he subtly twists later in the scene in order to play upon Anne's sense of guilt and obligation. Richard implies that he killed Anne's husband, Edward, because Anne's beauty had caused Richard to love her—and that, therefore, Edward's death is partially Anne's fault. This tactic culminates in the highly manipulative, and risky, gesture of Richard's offering her his sword and presenting his chest to her, saying she may kill him if she can. But, interrupted by Richard's speeches, Anne finds herself unable to kill him. "Though I wish thy death, / I will not be thy executioner," she says—just what Richard is counting on (I.i.172–173). In proving that Anne lacks the will to kill him, Richard himself establishes a kind of power over Anne. He demonstrates that she cannot back up her words with action, while he backs every claim he makes with swift and violent deeds.

In a broad sense, this scene is a demonstration of Richard's powerful way with words, which may be the most important aspect of his character. He wins Anne, a seemingly impossible feat. She herself, knowing that she cannot trust him, is nonetheless unable to resist his apparent sincerity and skillfully manipulative gestures. He engineers the entire scene to bring about the result he desires.

As the gleeful Richard says after Anne has left—in a gruesome spectacle of rejoicing that tends to reinforce the audience's loathing of him, "[w]as ever woman in this humour wooed? / Was ever woman in this humour won?" (I.ii.215–216). Richard then goes on to gloat over his murder of her husband, Edward, to which he now openly admits. Last, Richard seems to take pleasure in comparing his own ugliness to Edward's nobility—appreciating the accompanying irony that the beautiful Anne will now belong to the hideous Richard. It is difficult to read this scene without concluding that Richard is twisted in mind and emotion as well as body. His intelligence, his skill with words, and his apparently motiveless hatred of the world at large combine with these twisted emotions to make Richard very dangerous indeed.

ACT I, SCENE III

Thou elvish-marked, abortive, rooting hog,
Thou that wast sealed in thy nativity
The slave of nature and the son of hell.
(See QUOTATIONS, *p. 59)*

SUMMARY

Queen Elizabeth, the wife of the sickly King Edward IV, enters with members of her family: her brother, Lord Rivers, and her two sons from a prior marriage, Lord Gray and the Marquis of Dorset. The queen tells her relatives that she is fearful because her husband is growing sicker and seems unlikely to survive his illness. The king and queen have two sons, but the princes are still too young to rule. If King Edward dies, control of the throne will go to Richard until the oldest son comes of age. Elizabeth tells her kinsmen that Richard is hostile to her and that she fears for her safety and that of her sons.

Two noblemen enter: the duke of Buckingham, and Stanley, the earl of Derby. They report that King Edward is doing better, and that he wants to make peace between Richard and Elizabeth's kinsmen, between whom there is long-standing hostility.

Suddenly, Richard enters, complaining loudly. He announces that, because he is such an honest and plainspoken man, the people at court slander him, pretending that he has said hostile things about Elizabeth's kinsmen. He then accuses Elizabeth and her kinsmen of hoping that Edward will die soon. Elizabeth, forced to go on the defensive, tells Richard that Edward simply wants to make peace among all of them. But Richard accuses Elizabeth of having engineered the imprisonment of Clarence—an imprisonment that is actually Richard's doing (as we have learned in Act I, scene i).

Elizabeth and Richard's argument escalates. As they argue, old Queen Margaret enters unobserved. As she watches Richard and Elizabeth fight, Margaret comments bitterly to herself about how temporary power is, and she condemns Richard for his part in the death of her husband, Henry VI, and his son, Prince Edward. Finally, Margaret steps forward out of hiding. She accuses Elizabeth and Richard of having caused her downfall and tells them that they do not know what sorrow is. She adds that Elizabeth enjoys the privileges of being queen, which should be Margaret's, and that Richard is to blame for the murders of her family. The others, startled to see her because they thought that she had been banished from the kingdom, join together against her.

Margaret, bitter about her overthrow and the killing of her family by the people who stand before her, begins to curse all those present. She prays that Elizabeth will outlive her glory, and see her husband and children die before her, just as Margaret has. She curses Hastings, Rivers, and Dorset to die early deaths, since they were all bystanders when the York family murdered her son, Edward. Finally, she curses Richard, praying to the heavens that Richard will mistake his friends for enemies, and vice versa, and that he will never sleep peacefully.

Margaret leaves, and Catesby, a nobleman, enters to say that King Edward wants to see his family and speak with them. The others leave, but Richard stays behind. He announces that he has set all his plans in motion and is deceiving everybody into thinking that he is really a good person. Two new men now enter, murderers whom Richard has hired to kill his brother, Clarence, currently imprisoned in the Tower of London.

ANALYSIS

Richard's speeches in this scene display his calculated hypocrisy. We know that Richard has manipulated matters behind the scenes to have Clarence imprisoned and that he plans to ruin everybody else in the court and elevate himself to power. But when Richard enters this scene, he complains that other people have falsely accused him of evil actions. By boldly going on the offensive, Richard puts other people on the defensive and forestalls anybody accusing *him,* thus effectively managing to cover up his villainy. It takes a great deal of gall for the manipulative, rumor-spreading Richard to say of himself, "[c]annot a plain man live and think no harm, / But thus his simple truth must be abused / With silken, sly, insinuating jacks?" (I.iii.51–53). With these words, Richard accuses other people of conspiring to slander *him.* As Richard gleefully says at the end of the scene, he is so brilliantly hypocritical that he can "clothe my naked villainy / With odd old ends, stol'n forth of Holy Writ, / And seem a saint when most I play the devil" (I.iii.334–336). Here, as often, Richard seems reminiscent of the devil himself, who is renowned in literature for his ability to quote scripture to his own purposes.

Nonetheless, not everyone is deceived. Elizabeth seems to be well aware of Richard's hostility toward her, and their conversation, before Margaret interrupts them, is loaded with double meanings and subtle jabs. Furthermore, in her conversation with her kinsmen before Richard's entrance, Elizabeth seems to foresee the harm that Richard intends toward her family. She is savvy enough to be afraid of what Richard may do if he is named Lord Protector after King Edward's death, and, refusing to be cheered up by her kinsmen, says sadly, "I fear our happiness is at the height" (I.iii.41).

Margaret's extravagant and detailed curses, which she hurls at nearly every member of the royal family, create an ominous sense of foreboding. Since Shakespeare's world is Christian, we might expect curses, prophecies, and other forms of magic to be discounted as superstition in his plays. But curses and prophecies carry great weight in many of Shakespeare's works. Margaret hates the Yorks and the Woodevilles (the name of Elizabeth's family) because she feels they have displaced her and blames them for killing her own family. "Thy honor, state, and seat is due to me," she says of Queen Elizabeth, and she curses the royal family to suffer a fate parallel to hers (I.iii.112). Because her own son, Edward, was killed, she prays that Elizabeth's young son, also named Edward, will die. In addition, because Margaret's own husband Henry was murdered, Margaret prays that Elizabeth will also outlive her husband to "[d]ie, neither mother, wife, nor England's queen" (I.iii.196–206).

For Richard himself, Margaret saves the worst. After heaping terrible insults upon him, she curses him never to have rest. She warns both Elizabeth and Buckingham not to trust Richard. She says to Elizabeth, "Poor painted queen . . . / Why strew'st thou sugar on that bottled spider / Whose deadly web ensnareth thee about? / Fool, fool, thou whet'st a knife to kill thyself" (I.iii.239–242). The metaphors and similes with which Margaret describes Richard— "thou elvish-mark'd, abortive, rooting hog" (I.iii.225), for instance, or "this poisonous bunch-back'd toad" (I.iii.244)—refer to both Richard's physical deformities and his corrupt inner nature.

ACT I, SCENE IV

SUMMARY

Inside the Tower of London, the imprisoned Clarence tells Brackenbury, the lieutenant of the tower, about the strange dream he had the night before. Clarence says he dreamed that he was outside of the tower and about to set sail for France, along with his brother, Richard. But as they walked along the deck of the ship, Richard stumbled, and when Clarence tried to help him, Richard accidentally pushed him into the ocean. Clarence saw all the treasures of the deep laid out before him, as his drowning was prolonged for a very long time. He struggled to give up the ghost, but had to feel the terrible pain of drowning over and over again. Clarence then dreamed that he visited the underworld, where he saw the ghosts of those for whose deaths he had been partly responsible in the recent overthrow of the monarchy. In particular, Clarence dreamed that he saw the ghost of Prince Edward—the son of Henry VI and first husband of Lady Anne—whom Clarence himself had helped to kill. Prince Edward cried out aloud, cursing Clarence, and the Furies seized Clarence to drag him down to hell. Clarence then woke from the dream, trembling and terrified.

Brackenbury commiserates with Clarence, and Clarence, who has a foreboding of evil, asks him to stay with him while he sleeps. Brackenbury agrees, and Clarence falls asleep.

Suddenly, Richard's hired murderers enter unannounced. They rudely hand Brackenbury the warrant that Richard gave them—a legal document that orders Brackenbury to leave them alone with Clarence, no questions asked. Brackenbury leaves quickly.

Left alone with the sleeping Clarence, the two murderers debate how best to kill him. Both suffer some pangs of conscience, but the memory of the reward Richard offers them overcomes their qualms. Eventually they decide to beat him with their swords and then to drown him in the keg of wine in the next room. But Clarence suddenly wakes and pleads with them for his life. The murderers waver in their resolve, and Clarence finally asks them to go to his brother Richard, who, Clarence thinks, will reward them for sparing his life. One of the murderers hesitates, but, the other, after revealing to the unbelieving Clarence that it is Richard who has sent them to kill him, stabs Clarence, and puts his body in the keg. The murderers flee the scene before anyone comes to investigate.

> *O Lord! Methought what pain it was to drown....*
> *(See* QUOTATIONS, *p. 60)*

(See QUOTATIONS, p. 60)

ANALYSIS

Clarence's description of his dream is notable for both its striking language and its portentous foreshadowing. Clarence is unaware that Richard is behind his imprisonment, but he nonetheless dreams that his brother causes his death. His vivid description of the terror of drowning is also memorable: "O Lord! Methought what pain it was to drown / What dreadful noise of waters in my ears, / What sights of ugly death within mine eyes!" (I.iv.21–23). The evocative phrases Shakespeare uses, such as the descriptions of the strange treasures Clarence sees and the "[t]en thousand men that fishes gnawed upon" (I.iv.25), juxtapose earthly wealth and human mortality—a frequent concern of Renaissance writers. Some of the images used here, such as that of the dead men's skulls at the bottom of the sea into whose eye sockets reflecting gems have fallen, are similar to images that Shakespeare uses in his later play *The Tempest*. In that play, a fairy sings to a young prince whose father is believed to have drowned at sea, describing the way his father's bones have turned into coral and his eyes to pearls.

Clarence's dream is also an eerie foreshadowing of his actual drowning later in the scene. Moreover, it foreshadows the nightmare Richard himself experiences just before battle in Act V, scene v. Like the appearance of Margaret's curses in Act I, scene iii, the use of a foreshadowing dream here indicates the predominance of the supernatural in *Richard III*. While the play is technically classified as a history play, in many respects it more closely resembles Shakespearean tragedy, given its villainous central character, Richard, and the crucial role played by supernatural occurrences such as curses, ghosts, prophecies, and dreams.

When the murderers arrive, they debate between themselves before actually killing Clarence, introducing flashes of humor into the grisly scene. "[S]hall I stab him as he sleeps?" asks one, to which the other replies, "No. He'll say 'twas done cowardly, when he wakes" (I.iv.96–98). In a lighthearted tone that disguises a serious meaning, the hesitant murderer speaks later of the inconvenience of having a conscience: "A man cannot steal but it accuseth him . . . a man cannot lie with his neighbour's wife but it detects him" (I.iv.128–130). The use of humor in what would otherwise be an extremely grim and serious context indicates the dramatic complexity of the play. While, on one level, the evil of Richard and his murderers is unambiguous, Shakespeare nevertheless introduces significant psychological conflicts and subtleties.

When Clarence finally does wake, he comes very close to persuading the murderers to let him live, and in fact manages to hold them off for quite a while with his words. Richard's warning to the murderers seems justified: "do not hear him plead, / For Clarence is well-spoken, and perhaps / May move your hearts to pity, if you mark him" (I.iii.345–347). Eloquence is apparently a gift that Clarence shares with his brother. But, in the end, language does not save Clarence. His eventual murder comes at the same time as the revelation that Richard is behind his murder, an announcement that Clarence, with touching naïveté, refuses to believe (I.iv.221–234). Even after one of the murderers tells Clarence, "You are deceived. Your brother Gloucester hates you" (I.iv.220), Clarence falters, "O do not slander him, for he is kind. . . . It cannot be, for he bewept my fortune, / And hugged me in his arms" (I.iv.229–233). This refusal to believe that Richard could be wicked is a poignant illustration of just how convincing Richard's deceptions can be.

Act II, scenes i–ii

Summary: Act II, scene i

A flourish of trumpets sounds, and the sickly King Edward IV enters with his family, his wife's family, and his advisors. Edward says that there has been too much quarreling among these factions, and he insists that everybody apologize and make peace with one another. He also announces that he has sent a letter of forgiveness to the Tower of London, where his brother Clarence has been imprisoned and sentenced to death. (At this point, King Edward does not know that his other brother, Richard, has intercepted his message and has caused Clarence to be killed.)

With a great deal of urging, King Edward finally gets the noblemen Buckingham and Hastings to make peace with Queen Elizabeth and her kinsmen (Rivers, Dorset, and Gray), promising to forget their long-standing conflicts. Richard himself then enters, and, at the king's request, gives a very noble-sounding speech in which he apologizes for any previous hostility toward Buckingham, Hastings, or the queen's family, and presents himself as a friend to all. Peace seems to have been restored.

But when Elizabeth asks King Edward to forgive Clarence and summon him to the palace, Richard reacts as if Elizabeth is deliberately making fun of him. He springs the news of Clarence's death on the group. With calculated manipulation, he reminds Edward of his guilt in condemning Clarence to death and says that the cancellation of the sentence was delivered too slowly. The grieving, guilty Edward begins to blame himself for his brother's death.

Stanley, the earl of Derby, suddenly rushes in to beg the king to spare the life of a servant condemned to death. Edward angrily blasts his noblemen for not having interceded to save Clarence when the king himself let his anger run away with him. The already sick Edward suddenly seems to grow sicker, suffering from grief and guilt. He has to be helped to his bed.

Summary: Act II, scene ii

Later, in another room in the palace, the duchess of York, the mother of Richard, Clarence, and King Edward, is comforting Clarence's two young children. The boy and girl ask their grandmother if their father is dead, and she, lying to try to spare them, tells them he is not. But the duchess knows how evil her son Richard really is and that he killed his brother, and she grieves that she ever gave birth to him.

Suddenly, Elizabeth enters, lamenting out loud with her hair disheveled, a common sign of grief on the Elizabethan stage. Elizabeth tells the duchess that King Edward has died, and the duchess joins her in mourning. All four make ritualistic lamentations. The two children cry for their dead father, Clarence; Elizabeth cries for her dead husband, Edward; and the duchess cries for both of her dead sons—Edward and Clarence.

Elizabeth's kinsmen, Rivers and Dorset, remind Elizabeth that she must think of her eldest son, the prince. Young Prince Edward, named after his father, is the heir to the throne; he must be called to London and crowned. Suddenly, however, Richard enters, along with Buckingham, Hastings, Stanley, and Ratcliffe. Buckingham and Richard smoothly agree that the prince should be brought to London, but say that only a few people should go to get him, deciding the two of them will go together. All the others depart to discuss who should go to fetch the prince, but Richard and Buckingham linger behind. It is clear that Buckingham has become Richard's ally and accomplice. He suggests to Richard that the two of them ought to go together to fetch the prince and says he has further ideas about how to separate the prince from Elizabeth and her family. Richard happily addresses Buckingham as his friend, right-hand man, and soul mate, and he quickly agrees with Buckingham's plans.

ANALYSIS
Richard's calculated hypocrisy is demonstrated once again in Act II, scene i. He pretends to be a good person unjustly accused of harboring ill will, only to deliver the news of Clarence's death with a sense of timing calculated to send his brother Edward over the edge with grief, surprise, and guilt. Here again we see Richard's extraordinary unscrupulousness, his skill at lying, and his ability to manipulate other people's emotions. Richard's shameless hypocrisy allows him to say, perfectly convincingly, "'Tis death to me to be at enmity. / I hate it, and desire all good men's love. . . . / I thank my God for my humility" (II.i.61–73). It may seem strange that the noblemen believe him, but we have already seen how convincing Richard can be. Just as Clarence proves incapable of believing that Richard engineered his death even as the murderers sent by Richard prepare to kill him, so does Clarence's son, responding to his grandmother's suggestion that Richard ordered Clarence's death by saying, "I cannot think it" (II.ii.33).

Edward's long, angry speech at the end of Act II, scene i is his only major speech, and his last before he dies. It is unusually touching and powerful, and it appeals to the importance of loyalty and love over the maneuvering and flattery that prevails in the court. Edward asks why no member of his court reminded him in his rage of how much he owed his brother Clarence; he then asks why no one advised him to refrain from issuing a death sentence. He puts these questions succinctly: "Who spoke of brotherhood? Who spoke of love?" (II.i.109). Instead, the death sentence was issued, and, according to the story Richard tells, the letter of reversal that

Edward sent out did not arrive at the tower in time. Of course, Richard deliberately intercepted the reversal and sent the death sentence, along with his murderers, to the tower. Richard is too evil to be affected by Edward's eloquent words.

Unfortunately for the king, the effort of his speech and his guilt over Clarence's death seem to wear him out. The results of this stress on the already sick king are apparent in Act II, scene ii, in which we discover that Edward has suddenly died. The mourning scene of Elizabeth, the duchess, and Clarence's children is highly ritualistic. The formality of their language and the symmetrical structuring of their mournful cries shift the focus of the play away from psychological realism toward a more stylized and theatrical depiction of grief. The manipulations and maneuvering that go on at the end of the scene demonstrate that the death of Edward is to have more far-reaching consequences than may immediately be apparent. The imminent shift of power should, in theory, give the reins of power to young Prince Edward, the son of Elizabeth and the late King Edward and the next in line for the throne.

ACT II, SCENES III–IV

SUMMARY: ACT II, SCENE III

Three ordinary citizens on a street in London discuss the state of national affairs. They share the news of King Edward's death, and, although one of them is optimistic about the future, saying that Edward's son will rule, the others are very worried. These citizens insist that, of the king's sons, the oldest, young Prince Edward, is still too young to reign. They state that the two sides of his family— the kinsmen of Queen Elizabeth on one side (Rivers, Dorset, and Gray) and his uncle Richard on the other—are locked in a jealous power struggle. Moreover, they see that Richard himself is dangerous, cunning, and thirsty for power, and they discuss his villainous nature. The citizens complain that it would be better for the prince to have no uncles than to have uncles struggling over control of him and the country. They dread what the future will bring.

SUMMARY: ACT II, SCENE IV

Back in the palace, the cardinal, an ally of Elizabeth's family, tells Elizabeth, the duchess of York, and Elizabeth's youngest son that young Prince Edward has nearly reached London and should arrive within two days. The prince's mother, grandmother, and younger brother say that they are looking forward to seeing him.

Suddenly, the marquis of Dorset arrives with terrible news. He says that Elizabeth's kinsmen, Rivers and Gray, have been arrested along with an ally of theirs named Sir Thomas Vaughan. They have been sent to Pomfret, a castle where prisoners are held and often killed. The order to arrest them came, not surprisingly, from Richard and his ally, Buckingham. Elizabeth and the duchess realize that this news probably means the beginning of the end for their family. They wail for their loss—and for what is to come. Knowing that Richard means her ill, Elizabeth decides to take her youngest son and flee to sanctuary—to a place where, she hopes, Richard cannot come after them. The cardinal promises his support and hands over to Elizabeth the Great Seal of England, a highly symbolic artifact.

ANALYSIS

Act II, scene iii is what critics sometimes call a window scene, because it briefly turns away from the actions of the noble characters to give us a glimpse into the minds of the common people. Because almost the entire play focuses so intensely on a close-knit group of noblemen, this technique of showing us the thoughts of people in the street offers a new point of view and gives the play a greater sense of perspective. We learn from this episode that the commoners are deeply concerned about the results of the power struggle that they know is going on in the highest levels of government. This concern heightens the tension of the play and also reminds us that the effects of these court struggles are not confined to the royal palace. Rather, they have profound consequences for everyone who lives in England. Historically, this window scene also would have made the play resonate deeply with a large portion of Shakespeare's audience, many of whom were commoners who, like those in Act II, scene iii, worried about how the behavior of powerful men and women such as the nobles would affect their lives.

In Act II, scene iv, the younger prince's jokes and puns at his uncle's expense show us that, unlike Clarence's young son, this boy sees through Richard's schemes. We also see that he is precociously clever, fully justifying his mother's reference to him as a "parlous," or dangerous, boy, and warning that he is "too shrewd" for his own good (II.iv.35). As we see later in the play, Richard does not like the people around him to be too shrewd, for when people can see through his lies they become a threat to his schemes.

Elizabeth's response to the news of her kinsmen's imprisonment might seem an overreaction to somebody unfamiliar with the situation, but given the context, her cry of fear, "Ay me! I see the ruin of my house," is perfectly justified (II.iv.48). She knows that an imprisonment engineered by Richard is likely to lead to death, as it has already done for Clarence. But, beyond her fear for Rivers, Gray, and Vaughan, Elizabeth can also see the larger meaning of this action. With Edward out of the way, Richard has begun to use his power fearlessly and without concern for reprisal. Elizabeth is now frightened for her own safety, as well as for that of her two young sons. The heir to the throne is in a particularly precarious position, since Richard has good reason to want him dead. Elizabeth's decision to take her youngest child and head for sanctuary is the only rational response. The sole question that remains is whether even this maneuver can protect her and her family from Richard's unleashed malice.

ACT III, SCENE I

SUMMARY

With a flourish of trumpets, the young Prince Edward, the heir to the throne, rides into London with his retinue. His uncle Richard is there to greet him, accompanied by several noblemen, including Richard's close allies, the lords Buckingham and Catesby. Richard greets the prince, but the intelligent boy is suspicious of his uncle and parries Richard's flattering language with wordplay as clever as Richard's own. The prince wants to know what has happened to his relatives on his mother's side—Rivers, Gray, and Dorset. Although he doesn't tell Prince Edward, Richard has had Rivers and Gray arrested and imprisoned in the castle of Pomfret; Dorset is presumably in hiding.

Lord Hastings enters, and announces that Elizabeth and her younger son, the young duke of York, have taken sanctuary (taking sanctuary means retreating to within a church or other holy ground, where, by ancient English tradition, it was blasphemous for enemies to pursue a fugitive). Buckingham is very irritated to hear this news. He asks the Lord Cardinal to go to Elizabeth and retrieve young York from her, and he orders Hastings to accompany the cardinal and forcibly remove the young prince if Elizabeth refuses to yield him. The cardinal understandably refuses, but Buckingham gives him a long argument in which he says that a young child is not self-determining enough to claim sanctuary. The cardinal gives in, and he and Lord Hastings go to fetch young York. By the time they return, Richard has told Prince Edward that he and his brother will stay in the Tower of London until the young prince's coronation. Both princes are unwilling to be shut up in the tower.

After he sends the princes off to the tower, Richard holds a private conference with Buckingham and Catesby to discuss how his master plan is unfolding. Buckingham asks Catesby whether he thinks that Lord Hastings and Lord Stanley can be counted on to help Richard seize the throne. Although Lord Hastings is an enemy of Elizabeth and her family, Catesby believes that Hastings's loyalty to the dead King Edward IV is so great that he would never support Richard's goal of taking the crown from the rightful prince. Moreover, Catesby believes, Lord Stanley will follow whatever Lord Hastings does.

Buckingham suggests that Richard hold a council in the palace on the following day, supposedly to discuss when to crown young Prince Edward as king. In reality, however, they will scheme about how Richard can become king himself, and they must determine which of the noblemen they can count on as allies. There will be "divided counsels" the following day. First, a secret council will be held to strategize. Next, there will be a public one, which everyone will attend, at which those plans will be carried out (III.i.176).

Buckingham and Richard order Catesby to go to Lord Hastings, in order to sound him out and find out how willing he might be to go along with Richard's plans. Richard adds that Catesby should tell Hastings that Queen Elizabeth's kinsmen, who are currently imprisoned in Pomfret Castle, will be executed the next day. This news, he believes, should please Hastings, who has long been their enemy. After Catesby leaves, Buckingham asks Richard what they will do if Hastings remains loyal to Prince Edward. Richard cheerfully answers that they will chop off Hastings's head. Buoyed by his plans, Richard promises Buckingham that, after he becomes king, he will give Buckingham the title of earl of Hereford.

ANALYSIS

This scene provides further evidence of Richard's skill at manipulation and deception, but it also makes it clear that Richard's manipulations are transparent to the right kind of person. When Richard speaks to the intelligent young prince, the boy is clearly not fooled. When Prince Edward says, "I want more uncles here to welcome me," he reveals that he suspects Richard of having acted against his other uncles—which is in fact the case (III.i.6). The prince may be referring to Clarence, his actual uncle, whom Richard has caused to be murdered. Still, since kinship titles are rather vague in Shakespeare, he probably refers more directly to Rivers, Gray, and Dorset, although two of them are actually his mother's adult sons.

Richard's boundless hypocrisy promptly comes to the surface. He assures the boy that his mother's kinsmen were "dangerous," since "[y]our grace attended to their sugared words, / But looked not on the poison of their hearts" (III.i.13–14). When he adds, "God keep you from them, and from such false friends," the irony is vast. Richard himself, of course, has poison in his heart, and is a false friend to the young princes (III.i.15). That the boy is aware of this is suggested in his suspicious reply: "God keep me from false friends; but they were none" (III.i.16). Prince Edward implies that he knows who his false friends really are, and that he is speaking to one of them—Richard.

Buckingham's urging of the cardinal to "pluck" the younger prince from the safety of his sanctuary is obviously unconvincing on either moral or theological grounds (III.i.36). His argument is based on the idea that a child who is too young to understand the technicalities of sanctuary must therefore be thought of as too young to claim he deserves it. Buckingham is clearly misinterpreting the very aim of sanctuary, which is to defend the helpless, but the cardinal is willing to let himself be persuaded by Buckingham, who is backed by Richard's threatening power. The cardinal, alas, does not provide a very admirable example of a clergyman willing to stand up for the right. "Not for all this land / Would I be guilty of so deep a sin" (III.i.42–43), he says at first, but it takes only thirteen lines of argument by Buckingham to "o'er-rule [his] mind" (III.i.57).

The young princes seem to have inherited a family intelligence and quickness with words. The younger prince, the young duke of York, jabs at Richard deliberately when he says he will not be able to sleep well in the tower for fear of his "uncle Clarence's angry ghost" (III.i.144). His older brother responds, "I fear no uncles dead," and to Richard's pointed response—"Nor none that live, I hope"—the boy answers, "I hope I need not fear" (III.i.146–147).

Richard demonstrates his political acumen once more later in the scene, when he accepts Buckingham's suggestion of the "divided counsels" for the following day (III.i.176). He sends Catesby off with what sound like reasonable instructions to find out surreptitiously whether Hastings is likely to be swayed to his side. However, after Catesby leaves, when Buckingham asks Richard what the contingency plan is, Richard replies simply,

"Chop off his head" (III.i.190). Yet Richard wisely makes a generous offer to Buckingham a moment later, promising him an earldom when Richard obtains the throne.

Act III, scenes ii–iv

Summary: Act III, scene ii

Very early in the morning, a messenger knocks at the door of Lord Hastings, sent by Hastings's friend Lord Stanley. The messenger tells Hastings that Stanley has learned about the "divided counsels" that Richard plans to hold this day (III.i.176). The previous night, the messenger says, Stanley had a nightmare in which a boar attacked and killed him. The boar is Richard's heraldic symbol, and according to the messenger, Stanley is afraid for his safety and that of Hastings. He urges Hastings to take to horseback and flee with him before the sun rises, heading away from Richard and toward safety.

Hastings dismisses Stanley's fears and tells the messenger to assure Stanley that there is nothing to fear. Catesby arrives at Hastings's house. He has been sent by Richard to discover Hastings's feelings about Richard's scheme to rise to power. But when Catesby brings up the idea that Richard should take the crown instead of Prince Edward, Hastings recoils in horror. Seeing that Hastings will not change his mind, Catesby seems to drop the issue.

Stanley arrives, complaining of his forebodings, but Hastings cheerfully reassures him of their safety. Finally, Hastings goes off to the council meeting along with Buckingham. Ironically, Hastings is celebrating the news that Elizabeth's kinsmen will be executed, thinking that he and his friend Stanley are safe in the favor of Richard and Buckingham. Hastings is blissfully unaware of Richard's plan to decapitate him should Hastings refuse to join Richard's side.

Summary: Act III, scene iii

Guarded by the armed Sir Richard Ratcliffe, the queen's kinsmen Rivers and Gray, along with their friend Sir Thomas Vaughan, enter their prison at Pomfret Castle. Rivers laments their impending execution. He tells Ratcliffe that they are being killed for nothing but their loyalty, and that their killers will eventually pay for their crimes. Gray, remembering Margaret's curse, says that it has finally descended upon them, and that the fate that awaits them is their punishment for their original complicity in the Yorkists' murder of Henry VI and his son. Rivers reminds Gray that Margaret also cursed Richard and his allies. He prays for God to remember these curses but to forgive the one Margaret pronounced against Elizabeth herself, and her two young sons, the princes. The three embrace and prepare for their deaths.

SUMMARY: ACT III, SCENE IV

At Richard's Council session in the Tower of London, the suspicious Hastings asks the councilors about the cause of their meeting. He says that the meeting's purpose is supposed to be to discuss the date on which Prince Edward should be crowned king, and Derby affirms that this is indeed the purpose of the meeting. Richard arrives, smiling and pleasant, and asks the Bishop of Ely to send for a bowl of strawberries. But Buckingham takes Richard aside to tell him what Catesby has learned—that Hastings is loyal to the young princes and is unlikely to go along with Richard's plans to seize power.

When Richard re-enters the council room, he has changed his tune entirely. Pretending to be enraged, he displays his arm—which, as everyone knows, has been deformed since his birth—and says that Queen Elizabeth, conspiring with Hastings's mistress Shore, must have cast a spell on him to cause its withering. When Hastings hesitates before accepting this speculation as fact, Richard promptly accuses Hastings of treachery, orders his execution, and tells his men that he will not eat until he has been presented with Hastings's head. Left alone with his executioners, the stunned Hastings slowly realizes that Stanley was right all along. Richard is a manipulative, power-hungry traitor, and Hastings has been dangerously overconfident. Realizing that nothing can now save England from Richard's rapacious desire for power, he too cries out despairingly that Margaret's curse has finally struck home.

ANALYSIS: ACT III, SCENES II–IV

Stanley's dream of the boar is the latest of many supernatural signs and omens in the play. Given what we know about Richard, Hastings obviously would have been wise to pay attention to this omen. Instead, he dismisses it, due to his supposedly rational skepticism. "I wonder he's so simple, / To trust the mock'ry of unquiet slumbers," he says genially of Stanley (III.ii.23–24). Another factor in Hastings's easy dismissal of the dream, however, is his own inflated ego, which leads him to be overconfident and complacent. He believes that he and Richard are "at the one" in terms of their plans, and that his close friend Catesby will tell him everything that goes on in the second council (III.ii.10). He also makes one of the most egregiously incorrect statements about Richard in the play, indicating the depth of Richard's skill at deception: "I think there's never a man in Christendom / Can lesser hide his love or hate than he, / For by his face straight shall you know his heart" (III.iv.51–53).

Clearly, Hastings makes the wrong decision here, and when he realizes his doom in Act III, scene iv, he thinks back to previous omens. Stanley dreams not only that the boar destroys him, but also that Hastings's own horse stumbles three times on the way to the council "[a]s loath to bear me to the slaughter-house" (III.iv.86). "O Margaret, Margaret! Now thy heavy curse / Is lighted on poor Hastings' wretched head," he says (III.iv.92–93). We can interpret Hastings's fate as Shakespeare's statement that people ought to pay attention to the omens of their dreams, but we can just as easily read it as a warning against overconfidence. Hastings now regrets his earlier bragging about his enemies' execution at Pomfret, imagining "myself secure in grace and favor" (III.iv.91). Furthermore, he realizes that, if he had wised up to Richard earlier, he could have avoided his fate and perhaps even saved England from what Richard plans to visit upon it. "I, too fond [foolish], might have prevented this," he laments (III.iv.81).

Hastings also muses before his death on the "momentary grace of mortal men," an idea that the play returns to again and again (III.iv.96). The quickness with which people's fortunes can change was a very popular topic for literature of Shakespeare's period, and for good reason: in the courts of Renaissance England, a person's welfare—and his or her life—depended on the whim of the ruler. A shift in political power would regularly cause the downfall and mass execution of dozens of formerly powerful courtiers. Perhaps for this reason, Renaissance court literature exhibits a great fascination with the precariousness of human fortunes. The medieval idea of the Wheel of Fortune, in which those at the top of the wheel are inevitably brought to the bottom, and vice versa, was still very current in Shakespeare's day. This fatalistic view of human life coexisted with a strict Christian mindset that insisted that worldly belongings would cause corruption and could not buy glory in heaven. All in all, despite the burgeoning wealth and materialism of the Renaissance world, Renaissance people were often in great conflict about the real value and meaning of their money and their luxuries.

SUMMARY & ANALYSIS

In the moments before his death, Hastings muses on this theme. He reflects that the person who builds his hopes on material prosperity instead of God's grace "[l]ives like a drunken sailor on a mast, / Ready with every nod to tumble down / Into the fatal bowels of the deep" (III.iv.99–101). This idea is nowhere better illustrated than in the preceding scene—Act III, scene iii—in which we have a brief last look at Rivers, Gray, and their friend Vaughan before their execution. Hastings earlier rejoices over their downfall, but their execution is as unexpected as his own. Like Hastings, the doomed Woodeville men proclaim their innocence. Like Hastings, they recall Margaret's curse and foretell dire consequences for England under Richard's reign. Like Hastings, they predict that their executioners will face retribution for their deeds. "You live, that shall cry woe for this hereafter" (III.iii.6), says Vaughan to his jailers, and Hastings—in a similar mood—ends his last speech with a chilling couplet: "Come lead me to the block; bear him [Richard] my head. / They smile at me, who shortly shall be dead" (III.iv.106–107).

ACT III, SCENES V–VII

SUMMARY: ACT III, SCENE V

Richard questions Buckingham about his loyalty and his capabilities. Buckingham answers that he is able to lie, cheat, and kill, and is willing to use any of those skills to help Richard. Now that Lord Hastings and Elizabeth's family have been killed, and the court is under Richard's control, Richard and Buckingham know that they need to start manipulating the common people of England in order to ensure the crowning of Richard as king. The first thing to do is to manipulate the lord mayor of London into believing that Hastings was a traitor. Buckingham assures Richard that he is a good enough actor to pull off this feat.

The lord mayor enters the castle, followed by Catesby with Hastings's head. Buckingham tells the mayor about Hastings's alleged betrayal. He says that Hastings turned out to be a traitor, plotting to kill him and Richard. Richard tells the lord mayor that Hastings confessed everything before his death. The mayor, who is either very gullible or eager to go along with the claims of people in power, says he believes Richard and Buckingham just as if he has heard Hastings's confession himself. He says that he will go and tell all the people of London what a dangerous traitor Hastings was, and that Richard was right to have him killed.

After the mayor departs, Richard, very pleased with their progress, tells Buckingham the next part of the plan: Buckingham is to make speeches to the people of London in which he will try to stir up bad feeling against the dead King Edward IV and the young princes, implying that the princes aren't even Edward's legitimate heirs. The goal is to make the people turn against the princes and demand that Richard be crowned king instead. While Buckingham is on this errand, Richard sends his other henchmen to gather some more allies, and he himself makes arrangements to get rid of Clarence's children and to ensure that no one can visit the young princes imprisoned in the tower.

SUMMARY: ACT III, SCENE VI
On the streets of London, a scrivener (someone who writes and copies letters and documents for a living) says that he has just finished his last assignment, which was to copy the paper that will be read aloud to all of London later that day. The paper says that Hastings was a traitor. The scrivener condemns the hypocrisy of the world, for he, like everybody else, can see that the claim in the paper is a lie invented by Richard to justify killing his political rival.

SUMMARY: ACT III, SCENE VII
Buckingham returns to Richard, and reports that his speech to the Londoners was received very badly. Buckingham says that he tried to stir up bad feelings about King Edward and his sons and then proposed that Richard should be king instead. But, instead of cheering, the crowd just stared at him in terrified silence. Only a few of Buckingham's own men, at the back of the crowd, threw their hats into the air and cheered for the idea of King Richard, and Buckingham had to end his speech quickly and leave.

Richard is furious to hear that the people do not like him, but he and Buckingham decide to go ahead with their plan anyway. Their strategy is to press the suggestible lord mayor to ask Richard to be king, pretending that this request would represent the will of the people. Richard, instead of seeming to desire the crown, will pretend to have to be begged before he will finally accept it. They successfully carry out this trick, with various clever embellishments. Richard shuts himself up with two priests before Buckingham leads the lord mayor to him to give the impression that he spends a great deal of time in prayer. In a long and elaborately structured speech, Buckingham makes a show of pleading with Richard to become king, and Richard finally accepts. Buckingham suggests that Richard be crowned the very next day, to which Richard consents.

ANALYSIS, ACT III, SCENES V–VII

The king-making strategy that Richard and Buckingham carefully lay out and then implement is a brilliant example of political maneuvering and manipulation. But the plot is also likely to drive us wild with frustration, as we observe the transparent hypocrisy with which unscrupulous politicians can sway the course of nations. On the other hand, the scenes are also clever and convincing deconstructions of political hypocrisy on a massive scale, in which audiences are likely to recognize reflections of their own time and nation.

The lord mayor of London, with his easy suggestibility, provides an example of a citizen who believes everything he is told by politicians and is all too happy to overlook the holes in a story. Richard and Buckingham are not called to account for the execution of the well-liked Lord Hastings. Instead, they simply use Richard's strategy of taking the offensive with a bold lie. By telling the lord mayor that Hastings was discovered to be "a subtle traitor" who was plotting murder and pretending to be shocked and grieved at the discovery, Richard and Buckingham prevent the lord mayor from having a chance to consider that perhaps, instead, they themselves plotted against Hastings (III.v.35).

The lord mayor is also happy to accept their suspicious story that the "loving haste" of their men accidentally has caused Hastings to be executed before the mayor could hear his confession—a confession that the innocent Hastings, of course, would never make (III.v.52). By anticipating any potential disagreement and bringing up opposing arguments before anyone else can, Richard forestalls antagonism. When he expresses concern that the citizens "haply may / Misconster us in him [Hastings], and wail his death," the Lord Mayor assures him that "my good lord, your graces' words shall serve / As well as I had seen and heard him speak," and that he will tell all the citizens so (III.v.58–64). For the king-making spectacle of Act III, scene vii, Buckingham and Richard use this tactic again, as well as bringing in several other clever ways of manipulating the people's opinions. Richard himself brings up arguments as to why he should not be king, but Buckingham effectively counters these arguments, making it seem as if Richard is being unwillingly pressured into accepting the crown.

Richard's refusal to accept the crown at first makes him seem even more hesitant—and, according to the principles of reverse psychology, makes it seem more desirable that he should be prevailed upon to accept. This tactic is reminiscent of one that the Roman general Julius Caesar employed. According to legend (and as Shakespeare recounts in the play *Julius Caesar*), Caesar was offered the crown three times. He refused it twice, but accepted it the third time, to the joy of the people, who had of course been whipped into a frenzy of excitement by the tantalizing delay. Buckingham uses a rather crude analogy for the tactic, which nonetheless conveys the visceral sense of tantalizing excitement that lies at the bottom of the strategy. His advice to Richard is that he "Play the maid's part: still answer 'nay'—and take it," meaning that Richard should keep saying no, but accept anyway (III.vii.51).

The brief interlude with the scrivener, in Act III, scene vi, is another so-called window scene. Like Queen Elizabeth's kinsmen just before their deaths, the scrivener reflects on how transitory earthly happiness is: "within these five hours, Hastings lived, / Untainted, unexamined, free, at liberty" (III.vi.8–9). He also comments on the obvious falsehood of the manufactured accusation against Hastings, and thus shows us, as the citizens do in Act II, scene iii, that the common people can see through Richard's act well enough to be disgusted and frightened by him. "Who is so gross / That cannot see this palpable device?" asks the scrivener, showing that he clearly can perceive Richard's hypocrisy. "Yet who so bold but says he sees it not?" he ponders further, meaning that nobody is brave enough to say out loud that Richard is lying (III.vi.10–12). Like the citizens of Act II, scene iii, he perceives the direction that things are taking and is afraid of what will happen to England under Richard's reign.

ACT IV, SCENES I–III

SUMMARY: ACT IV, SCENE I
Outisde the Tower of London, Elizabeth, her son Dorset, and the duchess of York meet Lady Anne (who is now Richard's wife) and Clarence's young daughter. Lady Anne tells Elizabeth that they have come to visit the princes who are imprisoned in the tower, and Elizabeth says that her group is there for the same reason. But the women learn from the guardian of the tower that Richard has forbidden anyone to see the princes.

Stanley, earl of Derby, suddenly arrives with the news that Richard is about to be crowned king, so Anne must go to the coronation to be crowned as his queen. The horrified Anne fears that Richard's coronation will mean ruin for England, and says that she should have resisted marrying Richard—after all, she herself has cursed him (in Act I, scene ii) for killing her first husband. Her curses have come true. As his wife, she has no peace, and Richard is continually haunted by bad dreams. The duchess of York instructs Dorset to flee to France and join the forces of the earl of Richmond, a nobleman with a claim to the royal throne.

SUMMARY: ACT IV, SCENE II

Back in the palace, the gloating Richard—who has now been crowned king of England—enters in triumph with Buckingham and Catesby. But Richard says that he does not yet feel secure in his position of power. He tells Buckingham that he wants the two young princes, the rightful heirs to the throne, to be murdered in the tower. For the first time, Buckingham does not obey Richard immediately, saying that he needs more time to think about the request. Richard murmurs to himself that Buckingham is too weak to continue to be his right-hand man and summons a lowlife named Tyrrell who is willing to accept the mission. In almost the same breath, Richard instructs Catesby to spread a rumor that Queen Anne is sick and likely to die, and gives orders to keep the queen confined. He then announces his intention to marry the late King Edward's daughter, Elizabeth of York. The implication is that he plans to murder Queen Anne.

Buckingham, uneasy about his future, asks Richard to give him what Richard promised him earlier: the earldom of Hereford. But Richard angrily rejects Buckingham's demands and walks out on him. Buckingham, left alone, realizes that he has fallen out of Richard's favor and decides to flee to his family home in Wales before he meets the fate of Richard's other enemies.

SUMMARY: ACT IV, SCENE III

Tyrrell returns to the palace and tells Richard that the princes are dead. He says that he has been deeply shaken by the deed and that the two men he commissioned to perform the murders are also full of regrets after smothering the two children to death in their sleep. But Richard is delighted to hear the news, and offers Tyrrell a rich reward. After Tyrrell leaves, Richard explains the development of his various plots to get rid of everyone who might threaten his grasp on power. The two young princes are now dead. Richard has married off Clarence's daughter to an unimportant man and has locked up Clarence's son (who is not very smart and does not present a threat). Moreover, Richard gloats that Queen Anne is now dead—we can assume Richard has had her murdered—and he announces once again that his next step will be to woo and marry young Elizabeth, the daughter of the former King Edward and Queen Elizabeth. He believes that this alliance with her family will cement his hold on the throne.

Ratcliffe enters suddenly with the bad news that some of Richard's noblemen are fleeing to join Richmond in France, and that Buckingham has returned to Wales and is now leading a large army against Richard. Richard, startled out of his contemplation, decides that it is time to gather his own army and head out to face battle.

ANALYSIS

Now that Richard has attained the throne, it is more difficult to sympathize with him than it was before. He begins the play as a brilliant, driven underdog—a brutal and possibly psychopathic one, albeit, but an underdog nonetheless. After attaining his goal, however, Richard directs his actions toward securing and maintaining his power. We no longer feel any sense of suspense about when and how he will seize the throne. He has reached the pinnacle of success and must scramble to keep his prize in the face of all his opponents. Instead of using his skills at deception and manipulation to achieve clearly defined, difficult-to-achieve goals, he has started killing everyone in sight. As he notes, his goal is to "stop all hopes whose growth may damage me"—which amounts to killing everybody who could possibly be a threat (IV.ii.61). This new campaign of blood makes it much harder to find Richard attractive—even in the morbid, slightly perverse way in which we may be attracted to him earlier in the play.

This shift in Richard's personality—from self-assured confidence into paranoia—causes him to alienate Buckingham. Although Buckingham is the loyal right-hand man who has been with Richard since nearly the beginning of Richard's rise to power, Richard's wish to kill the children in the tower is something that repels even Buckingham. Whether Buckingham would have agreed to help Richard in the end, we cannot know, since Richard privately decides to drop Buckingham the moment he first hears him hesitate. This crack in the unity of his men is a turning point in the play—the start of a downward slide for Richard's fortunes. It seems that Margaret's earlier curses upon Richard ("[t]hy friends suspect for traitors while thou liv'st, / And take deep traitors for thy dearest friends" [I.iii.220–221]) are starting to come true.

Richard is determined not to let anything sway him from the course he is set on. As he ponders the idea of trying to coerce Elizabeth's young daughter into a marriage that will help secure his tenuous hold on the crown, he says to himself, "Murder her brothers, and then marry her? / Uncertain way of gain, but I am in / So far in blood that sin will pluck on sin. / Tear-falling pity dwells not in this eye" (IV.ii.64–67). These words contrast intriguingly with the Tyrrell's speech in Act IV, scene iii, which demonstrates that even a hardened murderer can have pangs of conscience. Richard's understanding of himself, however, leaves no room for such pangs—he sees himself as an embodiment of absolute evil and amorality.

Richard's complicated maneuverings accelerate in pace during the first part of Act IV, as he works to get rid of anyone with a legitimate claim to the throne. He has engineered the deaths of young Prince Edward and the young duke of York, the princes in the tower, since they are the sons of the late King Edward IV and thus the true heirs to the throne. He has already had his brother Clarence killed. Now, he has disposed of Clarence's two children by locking up the dim-witted boy and marrying off the girl to a lower-class man, to keep her from marrying a nobleman who might be able to use his wife's lineage to justify an attempt to seize the throne. Similar reasoning drives Richard to want to marry Elizabeth's daughter, young Elizabeth. Since she is the daughter of Edward IV, the last king, Richard intends to use her lineage to cement his own claims to power. (For similar reasons, it should be noted, young Elizabeth might also be a desirable bride for Richmond, the challenger from overseas and a relative of Henry VI who claims the throne by virtue of that relationship.) Richard muses that "I must be married to my brother's daughter, / Or else my kingdom stands on brittle glass" (IV.ii.62–63). Perverse as it may seem for him to marry his niece, prevailing Renaissance ideas about lineage and royalty validate such an action.

ACT IV, SCENES IV–V

> *Think that thy babes were sweeter than they were,*
> *And he that slew them fouler than he is.*
>
> *(See* QUOTATIONS, *p. 61)*

SUMMARY: ACT IV, SCENE IV

Elizabeth and the duchess of York lament the deaths of the young princes. Suddenly, old Queen Margaret enters, and tells the duchess that the duchess is the mother of a monster. Richard, she says, will not stop his campaign of terror until they are all dead. Margaret rejoices in this fact because she is very glad to see her curses against the York and Woodeville families come true. She is still as bitter as she has been throughout the play about the deaths of her husband, Henry VI, and her son, Prince Edward, and she says that the York deaths are fair payment.

The grief-weary Elizabeth asks Margaret to teach her how to curse, and Margaret advises her to experience as much bitterness and pain as Margaret herself has. Margaret then departs for France. When Richard enters with his noblemen and the commanders of his army, the duchess begins to curse him, condemning him for the bloody murder of his extended family and telling him that she regrets having given birth to him. The enraged Richard orders his men to strike up loud music to try to drown out the women's curses, but it does not work, and the duchess curses him to die bloodily.

Although shaken by this verbal assault, Richard recovers and, speaking with Elizabeth in private, broaches his proposal to her: he wants to marry her daughter, the young Elizabeth. The former queen is horrified, and sarcastically suggests to Richard that he simply send her daughter the bloody hearts of her two little brothers as a gift, to win her love. Richard, using all his gifts of persuasion and insistence, pursues Elizabeth, insisting that this way he can make amends to what remains of her family for all he has done before. He argues that the marriage is also the only way the kingdom can avoid civil war. Elizabeth seems to be swayed by his words at last and tells him she will speak with her daughter about it. As soon as Elizabeth leaves the stage, Richard scornfully calls her a foolish and weak-willed woman.

Richard's soldiers and army commanders start to bring him reports about Richmond's invasion, and as bad news piles up, Richard begins to panic for the first time. Richmond is reported to be approaching England with a fleet of ships; Richard's allies are half-hearted and unwilling to fight the invader. All over Britain, noblemen have taken up arms against Richard. The only good news that Richard hears is that his forces have dispersed Buckingham's army, and that Buckingham has been captured. Richard then learns that Richmond has landed with a mighty force, and he decides it is time to fight. He leads out his army to meet Richmond in battle.

SUMMARY: ACT IV, SCENE V

Elsewhere, Stanley, earl of Derby, meets a lord from Richmond's forces for a secret conversation. The suspicious Richard has insisted that Stanley give his son, young George Stanley, to him as a hostage, to prevent Stanley's deserting Richard's side. Stanley explains that this situation is all that prevents him from joining Richmond. But he sends his regards to the rebel leader, as well as the message that the former Queen Elizabeth has agreed that Richmond should marry her daughter, young Elizabeth. The other nobleman gives Stanley information about the whereabouts of Richmond (who is in Wales) and about the vast number of English noblemen who have flocked to his side. All are marching toward London, to engage Richard in battle.

ANALYSIS: ACT IV, SCENES IV–V

Act IV, scene iv presents the fulfillment of predictions made in Act I, scene iii. The main female characters of the play—Elizabeth, the duchess, and Margaret—are together again. This time, though, they are all in the same situation. All of the women have suffered loss, defeat, and the death of their children and husbands. The gleeful Margaret seems to feel that a kind of cosmic justice has been attained. To her, the death of Elizabeth's children seems a fair return for the murder of her own husband, Henry, and son, Edward. She tells the duchess, "Bear with me. I am hungry for revenge, / And now I cloy me with beholding it" (IV.iv.61–62). Margaret sees just retribution in the fact that nearly everyone who has died since her husband and son was either a participant or a bystander during the murders of her husband and son. We cannot help but see the irony in this vision of justice, as we see the recurrence of a few common names within the royal family. Thus, for example, the dead Edwards of the York family become clearly symmetrical with Margaret's dead Edward, from the Lancaster family.

The idea of divine justice comes to the forefront in this scene, as Margaret's curses have come true. Elizabeth, whom Margaret views as a usurper and an accomplice to murder, is now just as miserable as Margaret earlier hoped she would be ("Die, neither mother, wife, nor England's queen" [I.iii.206]). In Act IV, scene iv, Margaret announces the fulfillment of her curse, and her accuracy as a prophetess: "Thus hath the course of justice whirled about / And left thee [Elizabeth] but a very prey to time" (IV.iv.105–106). Justice has caused Margaret's curses to come true, and now Margaret can metaphorically lift off her "burdened yoke" of sorrows, slipping it onto Elizabeth's neck even as Margaret herself departs (IV.iv.111–113).

Convinced of Margaret's power, Elizabeth and the duchess ask her to teach them how to curse, and the duchess applies the lesson only a moment later, as Richard enters with his accomplices and noblemen. Richard's sound cursing-out by his mother can be seen as marking another step in the downward slide of his fortunes—as well as his control over his situation. Richard is as calm as possible when Margaret curses him in Act I, scene iii, but under the assault of his mother he is clearly embarrassed, awkward, and enraged. When his mother demands of him, "Thou toad, thou toad, where is thy brother Clarence?" Richard desperately calls for his musicians to sound a noise of drums and trumpets (IV.iv.145). Unable to answer the accusations, he can only drown out their words.

But, of course, Richard's ploy is not successful for long. The duchess has no patience left for her son, nor any love. She seems to agree with Margaret's statement that "[f]rom forth the kennel of thy womb hath crept / A hell-hound that doth hunt us all to death" (IV.iv.47–48). The duchess tells Richard grimly that he has her "most heavy curse," which, she prays, will wear him down on his day of battle, while the souls of the children he has murdered will give his enemies strength (IV.iv.188).

Richard recovers from this rather devastating attack, but the events that follow foreshadow his downfall. In the very long discussion with Elizabeth that follows, Richard's rhetoric is impressive. He uses tactics from gentleness to rage to urge Elizabeth to let him marry her daughter. It seems as if Richard may be successful, as Elizabeth departs with a promise to let Richard know her daughter's decision. Just as when he convinces the grieving Anne to marry him in Act I, scene ii, Richard seems here to have won over a hostile woman. But when we learn in Act IV, scene v that Elizabeth has, in fact, promised her daughter to Richard's enemy, the earl of Richmond, we realize that Richard has failed to win over Elizabeth; instead, Elizabeth has deceived Richard. As we watch Richard turn frantically from one lord to another at the end of Act IV, scene iv, forgetting what he has just said and changing his mind, we sense that the situation is rapidly slipping out of his control.

ACT V, SCENES I–II

SUMMARY: ACT V, SCENE I

The captured Buckingham is led to his execution by an armed sheriff. Buckingham asks to speak to King Richard, but the sheriff denies his request, leaving him time to ponder before his head is cut off. Upon discovering that it is All-Souls Day, Buckingham's thoughts turn to repentance and judgment, and he recalls the promises he made to King Edward IV that he would always stand by Edward's children and his wife's family. He also recalls his own certainty that Richard, whom he trusted, would never betray him and seems to be recalling Margaret's prophecy: "[R]emember this another day, / When he [Richard] shall split thy very heart with sorrow" (I.iii.297–298). Buckingham concludes that Margaret was right, and that, moreover, he deserves to suffer for his own wrongdoing— for breaking his vows, for being an accomplice to foul play and murder, and for his folly in trusting Richard, who has indeed broken his heart. He tells the officers to bring him to "the block of shame," and he is led away to die (V.i.28).

SUMMARY: ACT V, SCENE II

At the camp of Richmond's army, which is marching through England to challenge Richard, Richmond tells his men that he has just received a letter from his relative Stanley, informing him about Richard's camp and movements. Richard's army, it seems, is only a day's march away. The men recall the crimes that Richard has perpetrated and the darkness he has brought to the land. A nobleman points out that none of Richard's allies is with him because they believe in his cause—they stay with him only out of fear and will flee when Richard most needs them. Eager for the battle, Richmond and his men march onward toward Richard's camp.

ANALYSIS: ACT V, SCENES I–II

The action accelerates in the scenes leading up to the battle. Shakespeare paces the scene so that events happen and news arrives in quick succession, leaving little time for contemplation on the parts of the main characters. At the same time, these scenes reflect back on important scenes earlier in the play, revealing the consequences of past actions and the fulfillment of past prophecies. Just as Elizabeth, Margaret, and the duchess's reconsideration of earlier times in Act IV, scene iv prepares the ground for their extraordinary moral transformation in learning to curse, Buckingham's memory of Margaret's curse here prepares him for an equally significant transformation—his sudden desire to repent and accept his fate. Margaret's curse, written off as an eccentricity when it is first delivered, is now revealed to be an accurate instrument of prophecy, and thus assumes its full importance as an instrument of foreshadowing in the play. The re-emergence of the prophetic curse naturally carries with it an overtone of supernatural oversight, implying that God or fate controls the action of the play. In this light, Buckingham's declaration that his execution is due to the justice of God, who, he feels, is punishing him for having aligned himself with evil, brings the notion of moral justice into full focus in the play. This focus on moral justice anticipates the dissolution of Richard's unjust reign by redirecting the narrative toward the idea of just outcomes overseen by the will of God. Buckingham underscores this point when he declares, "Thus doth he force the swords of wicked men / To turn their own points in their masters' bosoms" (V.i.23–24). In other words, the justice of God requires that evil men will be undone through their own wickedness. Buckingham intends this point to refer solely to himself, but Shakespeare frames it as a moral generalization that points clearly toward Richard.

The sense of impending justice that Shakespeare introduces through the execution of Buckingham is carried over into Act V, scene ii, in which Richmond and his advisors' complaints about Richard's behavior amount to a moral indictment, a list of all the reasons why Richard's removal from power is the outcome that justice demands. The sense of justice, strength, courage, and optimism inherent in the frank and determined conversation of the rebels stands in direct contrast to the sense of corruption, death, and impending doom that clings to Richard's court. Richmond's advisors employ language of defiance and resolution that takes Richard's crimes as the impetus for the action that the rebels must take. For example, Oxford declares, "Every man's conscience is a thousand swords / To fight against this guilty homicide" (V.ii.17–18). Like Oxford's, each of the short speeches made by the men here revolves around the idea that Richard has been a murderous and oppressive king who deserves to be overthrown and that, as a result,

Richmond's army is morally unwavering in its quest to overthrow him. Whereas the lust for power characterized Richard's rise to the throne, the principle of justice now directs Richmond and his army to challenge Richard's wrongful rule.

ACT V, SCENES III–VI

SUMMARY: ACT V, SCENE III
In his camp, King Richard orders his men to pitch their tents for the night. He says that they will engage in their great battle in the morning. Richard talks to his noblemen, trying to stir up some enthusiasm, but they are all subdued. Richard, however, says he has learned that Richmond has only one-third as many fighting men as he himself does, and he is confident that he can easily win.

SUMMARY: ACT V, SCENE IV
Meanwhile, in Richmond's camp, Richmond tells a messenger to deliver a secret letter to his stepfather, Lord Stanley, who is in an outlying camp. Stanley is forced to fight upon Richard's side, but Richmond hopes to get some help from him nonetheless.

SUMMARY: ACT V, SCENE V

It is now dead midnight.
Cold fearful drops stand on my trembling flesh.
What do I fear? Myself?
(See QUOTATIONS*, p. 62)*

Back in King Richard's tent, Richard issues commands to his lieutenants. Because Richard knows of Stanley's relationship with Richmond, he is suspicious of Stanley, and is holding Stanley's young son, George, hostage. He has an order sent to Lord Stanley telling him to bring his troops to the main camp before dawn, or else he will kill George. Declaring that he will eat no supper that night, Richard then prepares to go to sleep for the night.

Stanley comes secretly to visit Richmond in his tent. He explains the situation, but promises to help Richmond however he can. Richmond thanks him and then prepares for sleep.

As both leaders sleep, they begin to dream. A parade of ghosts— the spirits of everyone whom Richard has murdered—comes across the stage. First, each ghost stops to speak to Richard. Each condemns him bitterly for his or her death, tells him that he will be killed in battle the next morning, and orders him to despair and die.

SUMMARY & ANALYSIS

The ghosts then move away and speak to the sleeping Richmond, telling him that they are on Richmond's side and that Richmond will rule England and be the father of a race of kings. In a similar manner, eleven ghosts move across the stage: Prince Edward, the dead son of Henry VI; King Henry VI himself; Richard's brother Clarence; Rivers, Gray, and Vaughan; the two young princes, whom Richard had murdered in the tower; Hastings; Lady Anne, Richard's former wife; and, finally, Buckingham.

Terrified, Richard wakes out of his sleep, sweating and gasping. In an impassioned soliloquy, he searches his soul to try to find the cause of such a terrible dream. Realizing that he is a murderer, Richard tries to figure out what he fears. He asks himself whether he is afraid of himself or whether he loves himself. He realizes that he doesn't have any reason to love himself and asks whether he doesn't hate himself, instead. For the first time, Richard is truly terrified.

Ratcliffe comes to Richard's tent to let him know that the rooster has crowed and that it is time to prepare for battle. The shaken Richard tells Ratcliffe of his terrifying dream, but Ratcliffe dismisses it, telling Richard not to be afraid of shadows and superstition.

In his camp, Richmond also wakes and tells his advisers about his dream, which was full of good omens: the ghosts of all of Richard's victims have told him that he will have victory. Richmond gives a stirring pre-battle oration to his soldiers, reminding them that they are defending their native country from a fearsome tyrant and murderer. Richmond's men cheer and head off to battle.

SUMMARY: ACT V, SCENE VI
In Richard's camp, Richard gives his battle speech to his army, focusing on the raggedness of the rebel forces and their opposition to himself, the allegedly rightful king. A messenger then brings the bad news that Stanley has mutinied and refuses to bring his army. There is not enough time even to execute young Stanley, for the enemy is already upon them. Richard and his forces head out to war.

ANALYSIS: ACT V, SCENES III–VI
These scenes are the psychological high point of the play, and the turning point at which Richard's downfall becomes certain. The play vividly dramatizes the contrast between Richard's character and Richmond's character, shifting its perspective back and forth between them six times. The leaders, in their respective camps, make almost identical preparations as they ready for the next day's

battle, but the difference between them can be seen in the way they go about their business. Richard speaks brusquely to his lords, and, as we can see, essentially is isolated from all human contact. As a result of his malicious nature, he kills anyone who becomes close to him, gradually destroying all his close human relationships. He is in power, but he is alone: his brothers, nephews, and even his own wife are all dead at his hand, his mother has cursed and abandoned him, and even the person who was once his closest friend—Buckingham—has been sent to execution.

Richmond, on the other hand, is gracious and friendly to both his noblemen and his soldiers. The battle speeches of the two leaders clearly show their different styles: Richmond asks his men to remember the beauty of the land that they are protecting from a tyrant, and the wives and children whom they will be making free. He reminds his men that he himself will die in battle if he cannot win, and that, if he does succeed, all his soldiers will be rewarded. In contrast, Richard simply mocks the enemy soldiers, calling them "a scum of Bretons and base lackey peasants" (V.vi.47). As Richard says to his noblemen before his speech, he believes that might makes right, and that "[c]onscience is but a word that cowards use, / Devised at first to keep the strong in awe" (V.vi.39–40). Very much Richard's opposite, Richmond claims to fight for honor, compassion, and loyalty—in effect, he fights on the side of conscience.

The effect of the ghosts' procession is something like having eleven bitter curses ("Despair and die!") cast upon Richard in sequence. When Richard wakes, he is shaken by a bout of self-doubt and soul-searching that is unparalleled in the play, and that many readers think is one of Shakespeare's greatest moments of insight into human psychology. Richard—the two-dimensional villain, the bloody "hell-hound"—is forced to look into his soul, and is terrified by what he finds there (IV.iv.48). His uncertainty as to what he finds within himself, more than the ghosts' curses, shakes him to the core.

Sweating and terrified, Richard asks desperately, "What do I fear? Myself? There's none else by. / Richard loves Richard; that is, I am I. / Is there a murderer here? No. Yes, I am" (V.v.136–138). With this sudden, horrible revelation that there is a murderer in the room, and that he is it, Richard is suddenly uncertain of whether to be afraid even of himself. His lines dramatize the realization that the ghosts have inspired—that he is a dramatically different person than he has imagined himself to be. He suddenly recognizes that he is a murderer. His statement "I am I" can be read as an effort to assert his own self-identity. After Richard realizes that he has become something that scares even himself, the divide between who he once was and who he has become is astonishingly clear. This divide threatens even his existence. Once he realizes that he is afraid of himself and that he is a murderer, his immediate question is whether or not he will kill himself. His answer is conflicted. Although he avoids this possibility by claiming that he loves himself and therefore would not kill himself, he realizes moments later, "I rather hate myself / For hateful deeds committed by myself" (V.v.136–144). In this scene it is very clear that Richard has moved beyond a simple, flat version of the medieval character, Vice, and experiences the deeply divided emotions that characterize real human beings.

In a strange, haunting, and even moving conclusion, Richard unexpectedly turns to thoughts of others, and grieves for his isolation: "I shall despair. There is no creature loves me, / And if I die no soul will pity me. / Nay, wherefore should they?—Since that I myself / Find in myself no pity to myself?" (V.v.154–157). With these words he realizes, angry and desperate, that he doesn't even sympathize with himself. Even after he manages to put aside his terror and resumes the semblance of his old arrogance, this sensation does not fade. Clearly, for Richard, the end is near.

ACT V, SCENES VII–VIII

SUMMARY: ACT V, SCENE VII
The two armies fight a pitched battle. Catesby appears on stage and calls to Richard's ally Norfolk, asking for help for Richard. Catesby reports that the king's horse has been killed and that the king is fighting like a madman on foot, challenging everyone he sees in the field as he attempts to track down Richmond himself.

Richard himself now appears, calling out for a horse. But he refuses Catesby's offer of help, saying that he has prepared himself to face the fortunes of battle and will not run from them now. He also says that Richmond seems to have filled the field with decoys— that is, common soldiers dressed like Richmond—of whom Richard has already killed five. He departs, seeking Richmond.

SUMMARY: ACT V, SCENE VIII
Finally, Richmond appears, and Richard returns. They face each other at last and fight a bloody duel. Richmond wins, and kills King Richard with his sword. Richmond runs back into battle. The noise

of battle dies down, and Richmond returns, accompanied by his noblemen. We learn that Richmond's side has won the battle. This revelation is hardly surprising, since Richard is dead. Stanley, swearing his loyalty to the new king, presents Richmond with the crown, which has been taken from Richard's body. Richmond accepts the crown and puts it on.

Relatively few noblemen have been killed, and Stanley's young son, George, is still safe. Richmond, now King Henry VII, orders that the bodies of the dead be buried, and that Richard's soldiers—who have fled the field—should all be given amnesty. He then announces his intention to marry young Elizabeth, daughter of the former Queen Elizabeth and of the late King Edward IV. The houses of Lancaster and York will be united at last, and the long bloodshed will be over. The new king asks for God's blessing on England and the marriage, and for a lasting peace. The nobles leave the stage.

ANALYSIS: ACT V, SCENES VII–VIII

Richard's death is conveyed only in stage directions in the text—uncharacteristically, Shakespeare does not even give him a dying speech. Richard's death comes as no surprise, however. His final scenes only enact the outcome that the play has already established as inevitable, both in terms of narrative shape and in terms of moral resolution. In broad terms, the first part of the play shows a gradual rise in Richard's fortunes and power. These fortunes peak and then decline dramatically. Buckingham's hesitation to help Richard kill the young princes in Act IV, scene ii, moments after Richard's coronation, marks the beginning of Richard's decline into paranoia and his gradual loss of control of the events around him. The duchess of York's curses and Elizabeth's deception of Richard in Act IV, scene iv confirm this downward slide, which reaches its low with Richard's nightmare—and subsequent self-questioning—in Act V, scene v. After all of these events, it is clear that Richard's death, which has been predicted and prophesied many times by many people, is only a matter of time.

Richard's final scenes do illustrate something of the frenzied self-ishness of his mind. Shakespeare depicts the gradual devolution of his bold and reckless fighting on the battlefield, as he goes from fighting to protect his power and his kingdom to fighting simply to protect his neck. Richard lacks the sense of higher purpose with which Richmond has been endowed, and thus he lacks the ability to die nobly. In the end, Richard is obsessed with his own self-preservation, as indicated by his cry of "[a] horse! A horse! My kingdom for a horse!" (V.vii.7, 13). In this moment, Richard clearly reveals his priorities. He would trade everything for a horse on which to improve his chances of surviving the battle rather than die honorably for his cause.

Richmond's final speech primarily serves a narrative purpose, showing that Richard, the villain of the play, has been definitively vanquished, although his death has occurred offstage. Richmond's simple, judgmental declaration that "[T]he bloody dog is dead" indicates the relief and exhaustion that he (and everyone else) feels after Richard's long campaign of cruelty (V.viii.2). Many dead kings, even wicked ones, are remembered kindly by their enemies after they die, but Richard is so universally hated that he is spoken of merely as a "bloody dog." Symbolically, then, Richard's death and Richmond's ascension to the throne suggest that the conflicts that have plagued England for so long are at an end. "England hath long been mad, and scarred herself," says Richmond, referring to the wars among the royalty (V.viii.23). Richmond's intention to claim the kingdom's "long usurpèd royalty," as Stanley puts it, heralds the symbolic end not just of the particular conflict with Richard but of the Wars of the Roses in general (V.viii.4). Moreover, with his marriage to young Elizabeth, Richmond will meld the houses of York and Lancaster in a fertile and peaceful union, uniting "the white rose and the red"—the symbols of the houses of York and Lancaster, respectively (V.viii.19). Richard's long reign of terror has come to an end as the play closes with the promise of a marriage, and with the new King Henry's fervent prayer for "this fair land's peace" (V.viii.39). The play, then, ends tragically for Richard but happily for England.

Important Quotations Explained

1.   Now is the winter of our discontent
Made glorious summer by this son of York;
And all the clouds that loured upon our house
In the deep bosom of the ocean buried.
Now are our brows bound with victorious wreaths,
Our bruisèd arms hung up for monuments,
Our stern alarums changed to merry meetings,
Our dreadful marches to delightful measures.
Grim-visaged war hath smoothed his wrinkled front,
. . .
He capers nimbly in a lady's chamber
To the lascivious pleasing of a lute.
But I, that am not shaped for sportive tricks
Nor made to court an amorous looking-glass;
. . .
Why, I in this weak piping time of peace
Have no delight to pass away the time,
Unless to spy my shadow in the sun
And descant on mine own deformity.
And therefore since I cannot prove a lover
To entertain these fair well-spoken days,
I am determined to prove a villain
And hate the idle pleasures of these days.
    (I.i. 1–40)

Richard speaks these lines to the audience at the beginning of the play. His speech serves a number of important purposes. It sets the scene, informing the audience that the play begins shortly after the death of Henry VI, with King Edward IV restored to the throne of England. Richard speaks of recent fighting, and says that "All the clouds that loured upon our house"—that is, the house of York— have been dispelled by the "son of York," King Edward, whose symbol was the sun. Richard paints a vivid picture in which the English have put aside their arms and armor and celebrate in peace and happiness, culminating in the image of the god of war smoothing his rough and fierce appearance and playing the part of a lover in a woman's chamber. All of these images make it clear to us that Richard has no justification for seizing the throne. England is obviously not oppressed or subject to tyranny, and Richard's own brother holds the throne. That Richard intends to upset the kingdom by seizing power for himself therefore renders him monstrously selfish and evil.

Richard offers a pretext for his villainy by pointing out his physical deformity. He says that since he was not made to be a lover, he has no use for peace, and will happily destroy peace with his crimes. We are not likely to accept this reasoning as a valid or convincing justification for Richard's villainy. Instead of making Richard sympathetic, it makes him seem more monstrous, because he can so blithely toss aside all of the things that the rest of humanity cherishes. At the same time, Richard's speech makes his true motivations seem all the more dark and mysterious.

QUOTATIONS

2.   Thy friends suspect for traitors while thou liv'st,
      And take deep traitors for thy dearest friends.
      No sleep close up that deadly eye of thine,
      Unless it be while some tormenting dream
      Affrights thee with a hell of ugly devils.
      Thou elvish-marked, abortive, rooting hog,
      Thou that wast sealed in thy nativity
      The slave of nature and the son of hell.
      Thou slander of thy heavy mother's womb.
      Thou loathèd issue of thy father's loins.
      Thou rag of honour, thou detested—
         (I.iii.220–230)

Margaret delivers this invective at the conclusion of her long dia-
tribe of curses against the Yorks and the Woodevilles. The speech,
and the scene that accompanies it, is extremely important to the
play, because it foreshadows the ends of nearly all the major characters, including the deaths of the queen's kinsmen and the fall from
grace of Elizabeth. Here, Margaret foreshadows Richard's end by
cursing him to mistake his friends for enemies, as he ultimately does
with Buckingham, and his enemies for friends, as he does with Stanley. She also curses him to sleeplessness, which he experiences the
night before the Battle of Bosworth Field, when the ghosts of those
he has murdered visit him. As a prophetic curse, the speech is one of
the most notable instances of supernaturalism in the play, and it also
contains some of the play's most forceful and memorable language
("Thou elvish-marked, abortive, rooting hog") in the form of
Margaret's insults.

QUOTATIONS

3.　　Methoughts that I had broken from the Tower,
　　　And was embarked to cross to Burgundy,
　　　And in my company my brother Gloucester,
　　　. . .
　　　Methought that Gloucester stumbled, and in falling
　　　Struck me—that thought to stay him—overboard
　　　Into the tumbling billows of the main.
　　　　　(I.iv.9–20)

Clarence delivers this speech shortly before the murderers come to kill him in the tower. Clarence says that he dreamed he escaped from the tower and fled with Richard ("Gloucester") to France, but on the ship, Richard betrayed him and cast him overboard to drown. This is the first of several prophetic dreams in the play, and it contributes to our sense that supernatural forces are at work driving the plot. Clarence's dream foreshadows his imminent death, as well as the fact that he will be drowned (in a barrel of wine). Psychologically, the speech is interesting because it reveals the depth of Clarence's trust for Richard. Rather than take this strikingly prophetic dream in which Richard betrays and kills him as an omen, Clarence refuses to credit the notion that Richard wishes him dead. To us it may appear that Clarence's unconscious mind is trying to tell him something, but if that is the case, Clarence's conscious mind is not listening. Clarence's disbelief in his own dream creates the impression that Richard's evil is too monstrous for those around him to accept or imagine, and thus it amplifies our horror of Richard.

4.   Forbear to sleep the nights, and fast the days;
      Compare dead happiness with living woe;
      Think that thy babes were sweeter than they were,
      And he that slew them fouler than he is.
      Bett'ring thy loss makes the bad causer worse.
      Revolving this will teach thee how to curse.
         (IV.iv.118–123)

Margaret makes this speech as she teaches the duchess and Elizabeth how to curse. Margaret says that to wrench the full power of anguish from language one must steep oneself in one's misery, staying awake at night, going hungry during the day, and even convincing oneself that one's children were better than they actually were. This speech is an important insight into the character of Margaret, who has made it her life to experience the pain of loss. It is also an important insight into the plight of victimized women in the play, who have no weapon against their victimizers but language and who must continually inflict psychological violence on themselves in order to wield their weapon as effectively as they can. When Richard appears in the middle of this scene, the women, one of whom is his own mother, turn on him with ferocious insults, indicating that they have internalized Margaret's advice and learned how to transform their pain into curses.

QUOTATIONS

5. The lights burn blue. It is now dead midnight.
    Cold fearful drops stand on my trembling flesh.
    What do I fear? Myself? There's none else by.
    Richard loves Richard; that is, I am I.
    Is there a murderer here? No. Yes, I am.
    Then fly! What, from myself? Great reason. Why:
    Lest I revenge. Myself upon myself?
    Alack, I love myself. Wherefore? For any good
    That I myself have done unto myself?
    O no, alas, I rather hate myself
    For hateful deeds committed by myself.
    I am a villain.
        (V.v.134–145)

Richard makes this speech immediately after his visitations by the ghosts; it is perhaps the only moment in the play in which he reveals any self-doubt, conscience, or regret for his brutal actions. Richard seems to wake up, and he is so full of fear that he is sweating. To calm his fear, he reminds himself that he is by himself and therefore safe. But he is seized with renewed horror when he realizes that he himself is the most frightening person he could be left alone with. He asks himself rhetorically whether there is a murderer with him, and he realizes that he himself is a mass-murderer.

Frightened, Richard tells himself to run away, but he realizes that he cannot flee from himself. He asks himself whether he is frightened of his own revenge against himself. This idea is very interesting—the forces driving Richard have always been mysterious, and here he seems to allude to some inner demon from which even he is not safe. But he quickly moves past this thought to assert that he could not hurt himself because he loves himself. However, he immediately realizes that he does not love himself, because he has never done anything good that merits love. Instead, he hates himself for the evil he has done to others. In the first speech of the play, Richard declares that he is determined "to prove a villain" (I.i.30). He now declares that he has become one ("I am a villain"). But rather than feel that he has achieved his goal, Richard is suddenly afflicted with moral loathing and self-doubt, a psychological undermining that may contribute to his downfall during the battle.

KEY FACTS

FULL TITLE
The Tragedy of King Richard the Third

AUTHOR
William Shakespeare

TYPE OF WORK
Play

GENRE
History play

LANGUAGE
English

TIME AND PLACE WRITTEN
Around 1592, London

DATE OF FIRST PUBLICATION
1597

TONE
Shakespeare's attitude toward Richard is one of condemnation and disgust, combined with a penetrating fascination with the mind of the power-hungry psychopath.

SETTINGS (TIME)
Around 1485, though the actual historical events of the play took place over a much longer period, around 1471–1485

SETTINGS (PLACE)
Various palaces and locales in England

PROTAGONIST
Richard III

MAJOR CONFLICT
Richard, the power-hungry younger brother of the king of England, longs to seize control of the throne, but he is far back in the line of succession. He plots and manipulates his way past the obstacles in his path to power, betraying and murdering with reckless abandon as he proceeds.

RISING ACTION

Richard persuades Lady Anne, Prince Edward's widow, to marry him; he has his brother Clarence murdered; he has the two young princes in line for the throne murdered.

CLIMAX

In Act III, scene vii, Buckingham and others entreat Richard to accept the crown, which he pretends to refuse and then accepts.

FALLING ACTION

Richard turns against Buckingham and murders the young princes and his wife Anne; Richmond defeats Richard at the Battle of Bosworth Field.

THEMES

The allure of evil; the relationship between ruler and state; the power of language; the rise of the Tudor dynasty in England

MOTIFS

The supernatural, dreams

SYMBOLS

The boar

FORESHADOWING

The play is full of foreshadowing, including Margaret's curses (which foreshadow almost all the future action of the play), Richard's monologues, the prophetic dreams of Clarence and Stanley, and the pronouncements of the ghosts in Act V.

STUDY QUESTIONS & ESSAY TOPICS

STUDY QUESTIONS

1.   *Is Richard the hero of the play or its villain?*

Richard is obviously a villain—he almost single-handedly generates all of the evil and violence in the play. But *Richard III* makes us reconsider our definition of what a hero is because, as evil as he is, Richard is certainly the play's protagonist. The entire plot is built around his struggle to become king and stay in power. We find out more about his mind and thoughts than about the mind and thoughts of any other character. In fact, Shakespeare intrigues us with the workings of Richard's mind and even asks us to sympathize with Richard's jealousy and pain, despite the fact that he is a murderer and a sadist. Richard is one of the most unsavory characters in literature, but his psychological depth invites us to try to understand his actions. The play thus compels us to explore our values. Even though we recognize Richard's actions as heinous, it is tempting to hope that he succeeds, and we are fascinated with the skill he demonstrates in manipulating other characters.

2.   *How does Richard's personality change over the course*
        of the play?

At the beginning of the play, Richard seems very much in control of
the situation around him. Bitter and alienated from others, he nonetheless enters into a close relationship with the audience, pausing
frequently to let us know what is going on in his mind. Richard
therefore has a closer relationship with us than he does with anyone
else in the play, at least in the early acts. However, as Richard's plot
unfolds and he rises in rank, his speeches change. He ceases to offer
monologues to us and is instead surrounded by noblemen all the
time. He also stops using his subtle powers of manipulation and
veers toward achieving his goals by force, ordering executions
overtly and no longer pretending to be a friend to all. Moreover,
almost at the moment of his coronation, he alienates Buckingham—
his only friend, whom he later has executed. Richard does not seem
to be able to return love; he solicits it only in order to twist it to his
own purposes, as when he seduces Anne, and when he attempts to
make friends with Elizabeth. Furthermore, he exploits the selfless
love of his family members to take advantage of them. By the time
Richard is finished, all his friends, lovers, and family either are dead
at his hands or hate him. This state of affairs leads to Richard's sudden revelation and nightmare in Act V, scene v, that "[t]here is no
creature loves me" (V.v.154).

QUESTIONS & ESSAYS

3. *What roles do women play in Richard III?*

Women play a number of different roles in this play, but these roles are for the most part defined by their relationships to men, and the capacity of the female characters to act is mostly frustrated by men. Young Elizabeth and Anne are wives or potential wives whom Richard tries to use as pawns to shore up his power. Queen Elizabeth and the duchess of Windsor are mothers who unsuccessfully try to use their influence to protect themselves and their children. Once Richard kills his brothers and Queen Elizabeth's kinsmen, Queen Elizabeth and the duchess become like Margaret—irrelevant and seemingly powerless. Interestingly, however, women seem to acquire power in this play only when they lose their male relatives— and, thus, their social influence and power in the court—and forge their own power out of grief and pain. This pain lies behind Margaret's terrifying cursing, and Elizabeth and the duchess try to learn the skill of cursing from her after the deaths of the Princes.

SUGGESTED ESSAY TOPICS

1. *What role does the supernatural play in* RICHARD III? *Why might Shakespeare have chosen to populate a play supposedly based on history with so many ghosts, curses, and prophecies?*

2. *How does the talent for wordplay affect the fortunes of the characters in the play? Is skill with words a sure sign of intelligence and capability, or does it indicate manipulative cunning and shrewdness? Why is the ability to express oneself so important throughout the play? Think especially about the characters of Richard, Margaret, and the princes.*

3. *Compare the characters of Buckingham and Hastings. How do their conceptions of loyalty to their respective masters differ? What traits lead them to their eventual executions?*

4. *How do the so-called window scenes, which show us the effect of the goings-on in the palace among the common people, broaden the focus of the play? How does the play portray the relationship between those in power and the masses of commoners whom they rule?*

REVIEW & RESOURCES

QUIZ

1. Whom does Richard blame for Clarence's murder?

   A. Buckingham
   B. Hastings
   C. Lady Anne
   D. King Edward

2. Who arranges the murders of the princes on Richard's behalf?

   A. Buckingham
   B. Tyrrell
   C. Hastings
   D. Clarence

3. How many kings does England have during the play?

   A. Three
   B. Two
   C. One
   D. Zero

4. What dignitary is involved in Richard's scheme to be crowned king?

   A. The high chamberlain
   B. The grand vizier
   C. The lord mayor
   D. The cardinal

5. To which house does Richard belong?

   A. York
   B. Lancaster
   C. Tudor
   D. Plantagenet

6. Which of the following characters is not one of Queen Elizabeth's kinsmen?

    A. Dorset
    B. Rivers
    C. Gray
    D. Tyrrell

7. Which character does Richard hope to marry in Act IV?

    A. Anne
    B. Young Elizabeth
    C. Margaret
    D. The duchess

8. On whom does Richard blame his deformed arm?

    A. Hastings's mistress and Queen Elizabeth
    B. Lady Anne
    C. Clarence
    D. Richmond

9. Why is it strange that Lady Anne would agree to marry Richard?

    A. Richard was previously married to Lady Anne's sister
    B. Richard killed Lady Anne's sister
    C. Richard killed Lady Anne's husband
    D. All of the above

10. What is Richmond's name after he becomes king?

    A. Henry VII
    B. Henry VIII
    C. Charles IX
    D. Sir Thomas More

11. What is Richard's heraldic emblem?

    A. The black rose
    B. The unicorn
    C. The sunburst
    D. The boar

12. Who delivers the curses that foreshadow many of the main characters' eventual fates?

    A. Queen Elizabeth
    B. Margaret
    C. The duchess
    D. The Witch of Shells

13. For what does Richard say he would trade his kingdom during the final battle?

    A. A horse
    B. A sword
    C. A gun
    D. A better army

14. To whom does Queen Elizabeth promise the hand of young Elizabeth in marriage?

    A. Richard
    B. Clarence
    C. Richmond
    D. John of Gaunt

15. Why does Richard order Clarence's murder?

    A. Clarence stands between him and the throne
    B. Clarence seduced Lady Anne
    C. Clarence is loyal to Henry VI
    D. Clarence is a Lancaster

16. To what house does Edward IV belong?

    A. The Yorks
    B. The Hapsburgs
    C. The Lancasters
    D. The Windsors

17. Whose son does Richard hold hostage?

    A. Hastings's
    B. Stanley's
    C. Richmond's
    D. Anne's

REVIEW & RESOURCES

18. What do the ghosts say to Richard?

    A. "Despair, and die!"
    B. "Wither, bloody villain!"
    C. "Thy death, and England lives!"
    D. "Fie on thee and thy house!"

19. Why is Hastings pleased when Elizabeth's kinsmen are executed?

    A. He realizes it will help Richard gain the throne
    B. He is jealous of the favor in which Richard holds them
    C. He is an enemy of the Woodevilles
    D. He will inherit their lands and their wealth

20. In what century do the events of the play take place?

    A. The fifteenth
    B. The fourteenth
    C. The thirteenth
    D. The seventeenth

21. In what prison are the princes confined?

    A. Newgate Prison
    B. Reading Gaol
    C. Folsom Prison
    D. The Tower of London

22. To what house does Margaret belong?

    A. Hatfield
    B. Lancaster
    C. Orleans
    D. Usher

23. To whom does Richard give his sword, claiming he wishes to be killed?

    A. Anne
    B. Rivers
    C. Clarence
    D. Richmond

24. How many ghosts curse Richard in Act V?

    A. Thirteen
    B. Twelve
    C. Eleven
    D. Nine

25. Why does Richard become alienated from Buckingham?

    A. Buckingham hesitates when Richard proposes killing the Princes
    B. Buckingham urges Richard not to marry young Elizabeth
    C. Buckingham defends Hastings at the council
    D. All of the above

Suggestions for Further Reading

BLOOM, HAROLD. *Shakespeare: The Invention of the Human.* New York: Riverhead Books, 1999.

BORIS, EDNA Z. *Shakespeare's English Kings: The People and the Law.* Rutherford, NJ: Fairleigh Dickinson University Press, 1978.

MORE, ST. SIR THOMAS. *History of King Richard III.* New Haven: Yale University Press, 1976.

POLLARD, A.J. *Richard III and the Princes in the Tower.* Stroud: Sutton Publishing, 1991.

ROSS, CHARLES D. *Richard III.* Berkeley: University of California Press, 1981.

SPIVACK, BERNARD. *Shakespeare and the Allegory of Evil.* New York: Columbia University Press, 1958.

WEIR, ALISON. *The Wars of the Roses.* New York: Ballantine, 1996.

REVIEW & RESOURCES